WAYS TO IGNITE
YOUR CONGREGATION . . .

PRACTICAL HOSPITALITY

D1124585

Randy Hammer

THE PILGRIM PRESS
CLEVELAND

The Pilgrim Press, 700 Prospect Avenue, Cleveland, Ohio 44115
thepilgrimpress.com
© 2009 by The Pilgrim Press

Scripture quotations, unless otherwise noted, are from the New Revised
Standard Version of the Bible, © 1989 by the Division of Christian Education
of the National Council of Churches of Christ in the United States of America
and are used by permission. Changes have been made for inclusivity.

Printed in the United States of America on acid-free paper

14   13   12   11   10   09   5   4   3

Library of Congress Cataloging-in-Publication Data

Hammer, Randy, 1955–
    52 ways to ignite your congregation—practical hospitality /
by Randy Hammer.
        p. cm.
    Includes bibliographical references.
    ISBN 978-0-8298-1825-3 (alk. paper)
    1. Church marketing.   2. Hospitality—Religious aspects—Christianity.
3. Church growth.   I. Title.   II. Title: Fifty-two ways to ignite your
congregation— practical hospitality.

BV652.23.H37 2009
254'.5—dc22   2008046298

CONTENTS

Preface · vii

Preface

I will be the first to admit that the idea of using simple tips to become a welcoming, hospitable church is an oxymoron —a contradiction in terms. As one who has devoted over twenty-five years to church revitalization, church development, and assisting small churches in becoming friendly and hospitable, I know as well as anyone that it is no easy task. In a day when the majority of mainline congregations are shrinking instead of growing, it is obvious that any program aimed at church revitalization, specifically the ministry of hospitality, is a complicated process. Just as it takes several different types of building materials to build a sturdy, aesthetically pleasing house, several different factors and the right conditions are necessary for church revitalization and transformation. Irrespective of church size, it is possible to identify some tips that can assist congregations in becoming more hospitable, welcoming, lifesaving stations for those who are seeking a church home.

What qualifies me to offer such information, you may ask? I admit that I have never been the pastor of a large church. I have spent my entire ministry working with small churches with an average worship attendance of 125 or less. But today this is where the majority of pastors find themselves. The so-called "megachurches" get most of the publicity these days, but those churches are few and far between. Most ministers and other church leaders are laboring in the trenches with churches that average fewer than one hundred in weekly worship. So this book is written for them.

Regarding my credentials, every church I have served has experienced growth in both attendance and membership. I bring over a quarter century of experience in pastoral ministry to the task at hand. I attended my first denominational church growth conference in 1978, thirty years ago, and I have attended more weeklong church growth conferences, retreats, and seminars than I could possibly count. From 1989 until 2002, I was the pastor of a new church development project. My family and I led in gathering, organizing, training leadership, leading a capital funds campaign, and designing and constructing a building. Additionally, I have been an avid student of church growth literature, and my personal reading list is extensive. Most recently I completed a doctor of ministry degree in congregational leadership. So, in this small volume, I have sought to bring together all the experience and wisdom I have gained over the years about how to develop a welcoming, hospitable congregation.

At the same time, as I share this material with you, I must readily confess my indebtedness to others, many of them pioneers in the church growth and church revitalization movement, upon whose work these ideas are based. Few, if any, of the ideas that are to be found in this program are original. In some cases I am able to cite where the idea came from. In many instances, however, I have simply recalled what I have picked up over the years by reading church growth and revitalization materials and attending church growth conferences, seminars, and retreats. I am indebted to well-known church growth leaders such as Charles Arn, Win Arn, Donald McGavran, Herb Miller, Lyle E. Schaller, and C. Peter Wagner. But I am also indebted to lesser known church growth devotees and practitioners who gave me guidance in church growth principles and new church development theory, namely, Jack Barker and George Estes.

I would be remiss if I failed to express some words of appreciation to the members of First Congregational United Church of Christ of Albany, New York, where the bulk of the material contained in this work took shape as the result of three years of intense study of how to become a more welcoming, hospitable congregation. My thanks to those faithful members who met initially on a twice-monthly basis, and then later on a monthly basis, as well as to the congregation as a whole who supported me in my ideas and emphasis upon revitalization and growth.

I present this material as one who has had a passion for helping small churches become more welcoming and hospitable, accompanied by revitalization and new growth. It is my hope that it will assist you and your church in doing the same.

PART ONE

Anticipating First-time Worshipers

"I was a stranger,
and you welcomed me."

MATTHEW 25:35

1

Understanding Your Purpose

ONE HOT SUMMER AFTERNOON, SEVERAL YEARS AGO, I WALKED INTO a little country store across the road from the rural church I was serving, took a soft drink from the cooler, and sat down at a table to rest. "Barbara," a woman in her late thirties who had been attending our church for a while, sat down at the table with me. As we talked, the subject of church attendance and membership came up. Barbara began telling me her story of defeat and how for years she had carried a great load of guilt over a failed marriage, divorce, and remarriage against the wishes of her former church. Barbara carried this great load of guilt, she informed me, because she thought that was the way God wanted it. She saw the guilt as appropriate punishment for her failure many years before. As I told Barbara of divine love, grace, and God's desire that she be set free of her great burden of guilt, she burst into tears and said, "You mean I have been carrying around this great load of guilt all these years for nothing?"

"Yes, Barbara," I replied, "I am afraid you have. We are meant to be free of the burden of guilt. We are given the opportunity for a new beginning."

To make a long story short, as they say, with some work of grace and some support, Barbara did let go of her great burden of guilt. She and her entire family recommitted their lives to things spiritual and became full, active members of that church. They became some of my best supporters. Eventually they were elected to important places of leadership. But the point I want to make is that, because of the pastoral ministry of that little country church, Barbara's life was transformed.

The first step for congregations wanting to become more welcome and hospitable is to understand what their purpose is. And after almost three decades of service in the church, I have come to see that the primary purpose of the church is to understand transformation. C. Kirk Hadaway, in his book *Behold I Do a New Thing: Transforming Communities of Faith,* poses the question, "Are people being changed (transformed) in my congregation?" Hadaway goes on to answer, "They should be changed into disciples who are open to the spirit of God and live a life of faith, vocation, and reconciliation in God's realm" (11). And so we begin the inquiry into the ministry of hospitality and welcome by understanding that our purpose is to bring about change, or positive transformation—in personal lives, the faith community, the community around us, and the world at large.

❊TIP:

Understanding your church's purpose is the foundation for becoming a welcoming church.

2

Writing a Purpose/Mission Statement

A PURPOSE OR MISSION STATEMENT THAT HAS BEEN LABORED OVER, written, adopted, supported, and publicized by the church leadership is imperative for a church that is seeking to be what it is called to be—a hospitable and welcoming life-saving station. The best resource that I have found to assist ministers and churches in designing a purpose statement is Rick Warren's best-selling book *The Purpose-Driven Church.* One does not have to agree with Warren's theological bent to appreciate all the good ideas he has to share with church leaders. The church's purpose statement should be posted throughout the building, publicized, printed in newsletters and bulletins, and mentioned often from the pulpit.

Everything a church does should revolve around as well as support that statement of purpose. All church programs and meetings, and even the church budget, should be judged in light of whether or not they support the church's statement of purpose.

Warren says, "What is needed today are churches that are driven by purpose instead of by other forces. . . . Strong churches are built on purpose!" (80, 81). A church's purpose statement serves the church in many different ways, as Warren points out:

- It builds morale and helps everyone know where the church is headed.
- It gets everyone on the same page—no one is at a loss in knowing what the church is supposed to do.
- It reduces frustration, since all know where they are headed.
- It serves as a polar (guiding) star for all the church plans to do.
- It allows concentration, as it helps focus on what it aims to do and what the church does best.
- It attracts others, as it lets potential new members know what the church is about.
- It assists in evaluation, giving something to measure by at the end of the year.

Three things should be emphasized about a church's purpose statement. First, it should be brief enough for people to memorize. Second, it should be faithful and true to the church's tradition (and the basis of their tradition), personality, and honest goals for the future. And third, it should include the element of personal and societal transformation.

The following is a sample purpose statement that could satisfy the above-mentioned points:

SAMPLE PURPOSE STATEMENT

The purpose of First Church is to share, in both word and deed, good news through worship, education, fellowship, outreach, and service to the end that lives, the community, and the world may be transformed.

TIP:

A Purpose Statement serves as a polar star for all a church plans and does.

3

Personal Invitation

While pastoring a previous fledgling new church development, our children got involved in Little League baseball. I took the opportunity to meet some of the other parents while we were waiting at ball practice. I began by stating my name and learning the names of those I was hoping to meet. After a while, I took the opportunity to ask each new person whom I met what line of work he or she was in. In other words, I showed a genuine interest in them. Eventually they got around to asking me what type of work I did. At that point I shared that I was a minister and that I was starting a new church in our community. Of course, I eventually issued a nonthreatening invitation to them to worship with us. To make a long story short, three of the families visited our new congregation, and two of the families became active, charter members.

One of the best ways to welcome new persons to your church is the old tried and true way—by encouraging and training current members to invite others to worship with them. They can also invite those who are new to the church or those who have not attended church in many years to attend a church function that would perhaps be considered less threatening than a church service. In the New Testament gospel of John, there is a story of how Philip, after commencing to follow Jesus, went and found his friend Nathanael and invited him to come and see Jesus. Upon meeting Jesus for himself, Nathanael was so impressed that he also became a follower and disciple of Jesus. Today in the city of Cana, there is a beautiful church named in Nathanael's honor. If only he could have known the legacy he would leave. And it was all because Philip issued the invitation to come and see (John 1:43–46).

When my family finds a dentist or physician that we love, we may be anxious to share that information with a friend or neighbor. Why should there be any difference when it comes to our church, and possibly a pastor, that we love so dearly?

Church growth expert Herb Miller, in *How to Build a Magnetic Church*, notes, "Churches that aggressively seek new members tend to grow." This holds true whether a church is conservative or liberal in its approach and theology. Miller contends that the one word that differentiates growing churches from nongrowing churches is "invite." "When a church isn't growing," Miller observes, "its members are not 'inviting.'" No amount of publicity can compare with a congregation in which the members are inviting their friends, relatives, neighbors, coworkers, and other acquaintances to join them for worship.

Citing another church growth expert, Lyle Schaller, Miller notes that people tend to invite others to church when their own faith is growing, when they like their pastor, and when they are excited about what is happening in their congregation. Evangelism (sharing the good news) is not just a responsibility of an evangelism committee. Evangelism, reaching out, and welcoming others must involve the entire church. Think of the positive results if every active member were to bring just one more new member into the life of the church in the coming months. In just a year's time, the attendance and active membership would double. How many lives would be blessed!

It is not difficult to invite someone to church. It is as easy as saying, "I was wondering, do you regularly attend a local church?" If the answer is "No," then the natural follow-up is,

"I would like to invite you to attend our worship service and see what we have to offer." This is the easiest but also most important thing a church member can do.

Elmer Towns has devised a program called "Bringing FRANC to Church." FRANC is an acronym, of course, standing for "Friends, Relatives, Associates, Neighbors and Coworkers." These are the people with whom all of us already have a degree of influence. It is only natural that we take the opportunity to invite them to church. When asked why they started attending a new church, a high percentage of members say it was because a friend, relative, neighbor, or coworker invited them. This brings us to Friend Day.

✳TIP:

*When asked why they started attending a new church,
a high percentage of members say it was because a friend,
relative, neighbor, or coworker invited them.*

Friend Day

"ALLISON," ONE OF OUR MEMBERS, HAD APPROACHED "LISA" AND "Lannie" on a number of occasions about visiting our church. Sometimes Allison would ask them, "Are you attending church anywhere now?" And Lisa and Lannie would have to admit that they were not. But then we planned a "Friend Day." We printed invitations and encouraged our members to invite their friends to church on that day. Naturally Allison sent Lisa and Lannie an invitation and followed up with a phone call. When they received an invitation, they said to one another, "How can we not accept

Allison's invitation to join her for services on Friend Day?" Well, Lisa and Lannie came, enjoyed the service and the fellowship afterwards, and even saw relatives whom they did not know were members of our church. They returned again and again and again. They met with me for new member orientation and united with our church about seven months after their first visit. And they (and the church as a whole) could not be happier.

It is obvious that a good excuse for members to invite their friends, relatives, acquaintances, neighbors, and coworkers to church is when their congregation plans a Friend Day. I have found that some members will invite their friends on Friend Day when they will no other time. Such a special day gives them the excuse to do so. And some people will come on Friend Day who will come no other time. Many come for no other reason than to do a favor for their friend who happens to be a member of your church. I could cite examples of former church members who were too timid to invite anyone to come to church—until we planned Friend Day. And by the same token, I could cite new members who were asked numerous times to visit our church, but didn't do so until Friend Day. If planned properly, Friend Day can be a life-changing experience for all concerned.

But for a Friend Day to be successful, some advance planning is necessary. A date should be chosen and cleared on the church calendar a number of weeks in advance. Perhaps it should be a special day of sorts, such as Thanksgiving Sunday, when thanks can be offered for the gift of friends, or Valentine's Sunday, when Christian love can be celebrated. Invitations should be printed and distributed for members to use to invite their special guests on that day (see appendix A). And a special coffee hour, fellowship time with refreshments, or luncheon should be planned after the service as a way to encourage visitors to mingle and learn what a great bunch of folks attend your church. Of course, all first-time visitors should receive a follow-up thank-you note from the pastor for attending and a brief follow-up visit from the church's welcoming team. For more detailed information on Friend Day, I encourage you to check out the Friend Day materials designed by Elmer Towns and Charles R. Schumate in their respective books listed in the bibliography section.

✱TIP:
Some members will invite their friends on Friend Day
when they will no other time.

5

Newspaper Ads and Articles

IF YOUR CHURCH HAS THE FINANCIAL MEANS TO DO SO, YOU MAY want to invest in a weekly, monthly, or at least seasonal newspaper ad that offers a positive, inviting message to the community. Since newspaper advertising is, however, quite expensive, the least churches can do is make sure that their church's name is listed in any free church listings. Perhaps the best newspaper "advertisement" is a feature story. Such a story can focus on the church's history, a special program, event, long-time member, or something else of interest to the general public. Many newspaper reporters will be interested in the opportunity to write about an important or historic event of interest to the local community. Feature stories can be supplemented with special block ads, say, at Christmas, Easter, or Thanksgiving. Our church has been featured on more than one occasion because of the stories of long-time members. Other opportunities for feature stories are when the congregation is planning some unique service or program. Still another example is when a church sends a group on a mission trip. The possibilities are endless.

I have noticed that a few churches tend to get a lot of newspaper coverage (the local Unitarian Universalist congregation being one of them!). One can only surmise that they do so because they are regular and persistent in submitting material about what is happening in their church. After a while, as newspaper readers keep seeing the name of the same church, week after week, they begin to think that something good must be happening there. At least some visitors who might not have considered visiting a church have done so because they saw the church's name in the newspaper.

✴TIP:

As newspaper readers continue to see news about the same church week after week, they begin to think that something good must be happening there.

Newspaper Flyers (Inserts)

AKIN TO ACTUAL NEWSPAPER ADS ARE NEWSPAPER FLYERS OR INSERTS (see Appendix A). In some cities, we see more and more of these inserts. People are obviously learning that this is a very effective and economical way of getting their message across to the community. Some churches are using newspaper inserts on a regular basis. The cost for an insert in one newspaper for example, is approximately $500 for 10,000 newspaper inserts. I suggest an 8.5 x 11, colored stock (perhaps agreeing with the liturgical color of the season) insert that says in state-of-the-art graphics what you want the community to know about your church.

To give you an example, about a week after our congregation had an insert placed in our local newspaper, I had an appointment with a surgeon to discuss a possible surgery. We had not met previously. When the surgeon entered the examining room and saw my name and what I did, she said, "Oh, that's the church that had the blue flyer in the newspaper last week. That was a nice looking flyer." I am sorry to say that my new surgeon did not come to our church as her family was already actively involved in a local congregation. But the flyer had caught her attention and did open the door for a lot of theological discussion. Fortunately, we did have some first-time visitors come because of these inserts.

TIP:

*Placing flyers, or inserts, in newspapers
is an effective way to reach the community.*

Community Visitation

THIRTY YEARS AGO, I BEGAN MY MINISTRY TO SMALL CHURCHES WITH community pastoral visitations. I understood that this was a natural part of the program. I led in gathering a new church development by knocking on doors and inviting people to consider visiting our new congregation. Over the years, I have knocked on more doors than I would care to count—several thousand, I am sure. Some pastors and lay leaders are more comfortable than others with the idea of making "cold calls" by knocking on doors. I can't say that knocking on doors is one of the activities that I have enjoyed most. But at various times, I have felt it was the right thing to do as a means of outreach to the community. Pastoral visitation in the community can let the neighborhood know that the minister cares and the church cares.

On the other hand, some communities are more receptive to having a minister knock on their doors than are other communities. There are some places in America where such a practice would be totally unacceptable, while there are other places (as in some rural communities) where it is expected. I am finding that more and more people are interested in having a "pastoral visit" to consider church membership either in the pastor's office/study or at a local coffee shop, rather than in their homes.

Communities also change over time. When our family arrived in middle Tennessee in the fall of 1989 to start gathering a new congregation from scratch, I found 98 percent of the population to be very courteous and receptive to my calls. (Although I knocked on all those doors, I can only recall a couple of times when the resident was rude and refused to hear what I had to say.) But by the time we left in 2002, it was a different atmosphere. It was obvious that not nearly as many were comfortable with a minister showing up on their doorstep uninvited, or at all, for that matter. So pastors will have to use their best judgment in their own communities of service.

Should one decide to do some cold community calling, a script similar to this might be adapted: "Hello, my name is Randy Hammer, and I am the minister of First Church. I am just trying to get acquainted with the community and see if there is any way we might be of service to you and/or your family (in the event that a suggestion is given, be sure to hear it and write it down, letting the person know it is important to you). If you don't have a church home at present, we would love to have you visit with us. Our service times are _____ . If I could, I would like to leave one of my calling cards just in case you should ever want to contact me. Thank you for your time." Every so often a contact is made through such cold calling that makes it all worthwhile.

✳**TIP:**
*Community visitation can let the neighborhood
know the church cares.*

8

Telephoning

In the late 1980s and early 1990s, evangelism by telephone was the hottest trend going. "The Phone's for You" was a program devised by Norman W. Whan of the Society of Friends primarily for those launching a new church start. The way it often worked was volunteers from supporting congregations received training about how to make an effective evangelistic call. Volunteers would be coached in asking respondents if they would be interested in learning more about a new church being planned for their community. A bank of phones would be set up in a sponsoring church or sympathetic business, and for several nights thousands of calls would be made from the local phonebook. It was not uncommon for two hundred or more first-time worshipers to show up for the opening worship service, constituting a new church from nothing. Not all of those who showed up for the first service would become members, of course, but many of them did.

However, as the telemarketing craze grew, and people got more and more tired of having their dinner interrupted by pushy salespersons trying to sell them something, the effectiveness of telemarketing evangelism began to wane. And then along came answering machines and voice mail not just for the purpose of getting missed messages but also to screen calls. This was followed by caller ID.

Nevertheless, the telephone continues to be an important means of communication for all of us, and its potential should be utilized to its fullest. Especially churches in rural areas or small towns might benefit from church volunteers gathering a few nights to call every household in their area to extend a well-scripted invitation to services or some special event. Even if an answering machine picks up, a positive message can be left that might lead to someone new giving your church a try.

In the new church development that we led in gathering, we did not use "The Phone's for You" program for gathering a church. However, using the Crisscross Street Index we did do some telephoning to the residents around the area of our church. I met one of our finest member families—one of those members became one of the leading lay leaders in that congregation—because of a random telephone call. So again, you just never know what might work.

✻**TIP:**

The telephone can be utilized to convey
a positive message about your church.

Special Programs and Events

SOME PEOPLE, ESPECIALLY THOSE WHO MAY HAVE LITTLE OR NO church background, are very intimidated at the thought of entering an unfamiliar church for a worship service. After all, there is an extreme diversity in the way that Americans worship, from the rousing, emotionally charged Pentecostal service in the South to the sedate, intellectual Unitarian service in New England, and everything in between. Someone who has no experience or background in different churches and the ways they worship may feel very threatened by the idea of entering a church for worship.

So, for many persons an invitation to some other special function—a children's Christmas pageant, ice cream social, quilting circle, potluck supper, computer club, book discussion group—may hold much more appeal and potential for actually getting some new visitors on your church property for the first time. I recall that when we were struggling to enlist new members in the fledgling congregation our family led in gathering, we held a fall barbecue supper. There was really nothing religious about it. One of our members was a restaurant owner and caterer who specialized in southern barbecue. Another of our members happened to invite Jim, a next-door neighbor, to come with him to the barbecue. Though he had a wife and two sons, Jim came to the barbecue alone. The next morning Jim showed up for worship. The following Sunday Jim returned for worship, bringing his family with him. Jim's family became charter members of our new church. He was elected to positions of leadership. And some fifteen years later, Jim and his family remained active members of that church, all because one of our members invited him to a barbecue where he was able to get acquainted with me, the pastor, and some of our members.

TIP:

Special events have potential for welcoming newcomers.

10

Outdoor Banners

COLORFUL, ATTRACTIVE, EYE-CATCHING OUTDOOR BANNERS CAN convey a sense of hospitality and welcome in a number of ways. Carefully designed vinyl banners that can withstand the elements are an excellent form of outdoor outreach. I have used a variety of banners over the years to attract the attention of passersby and to advertise special events—a new building program, Vacation Church School, a consignment sale, a fish fry, and most recently our denomination's outreach identity campaign ("God Is Still Speaking"). Soon after our church had hung the red banner with black lettering (to match our denominational outreach materials) between the white columns and over the doors to our sanctuary, a first-time visitor looked up and read the message, tears coming to his eyes. "I realized," the man testified, "that the message on the banner is exactly where I am on my spiritual journey. I immediately felt right at home." Six months later the man joined our church.

Vinyl banners can be purchased for less than $200. If one person finds a place in your church because of it, it will have been well worth it and will pay for itself many times over.

✳TIP:
Eye-catching banners can convey a sense of welcome.

Attractive Signage

I ONCE WAS INVITED TO PREACH ONE OF THREE SERVICES OF renewal at a small rural church. Along with two other ministers in the area who had seen growth in their churches, we were asked to offer a sermon that might be of help to this congregation that was losing members and struggling to survive. In the course of my sermon, I threw out some ideas that might be considered as avenues to revitalization and growth. One of my suggestions had to do with their church signage. The main sign was at least two decades old. The paint was faded and the metal was rusted. Red rust stains had marred the message. There were no flowers or shrubs around the sign. It was on a hillside where tall grass and weeds had grown up. I gently suggested that a new sign properly landscaped would be one good way to attract attention, as the church, though averaging only about thirty in worship, was on a major highway. Well, when I drove by the church a year or so later, I am sorry to say, the same old faded, rusted, sign surrounded by grass and weeds, was still there bearing the same message it had for years: *This church isn't doing much; it doesn't even care enough to update its sign.*

Though a new sign is certainly not a fix-all when it comes to church outreach, it can make a big difference. Some will want a sign that bears a permanent message, including the church's name (and possibly denominational affiliation), service times, possibly the minister's name, and the church's website. Others may prefer a sign that includes space for a weekly message such as the upcoming Sunday's sermon title or a thought provoking saying for the week. The sign, in my opinion, should compliment the church's building and be in keeping with the community where it is located. One of the plastic, lighted signs on wheels with flashing lights won't be suitable for every neighborhood! In any case, much thought should be put into the construction of a sign and the church shouldn't skimp financially for such an important investment.

A church's sign is the first encounter and first impression that most people will have of a congregation. How important it is that that first encounter and impression be a positive, inviting one. This leads us to our next point.

✸TIP:
*Much thought and consideration should be put
into a church's outdoor sign.*

Beautifying Church and Grounds

ONE OF THE THINGS I LEARNED EARLY ON FROM DR. ROBERT Schuller's Crystal Cathedral of Garden Grove, California, is that beauty attracts. If you have ever been to the Crystal Cathedral campus, or even seen it on television, you know that Dr. Schuller practices what he preaches in this regard. And his emphasis on beauty has surely had a positive impact on the growth of his ministry. All of us love beauty and are moved by beauty, and when it comes to the ministry of the church we should make every possible use of it. Landscaping with colorful flowers and attractive shrubs is important in and of itself, for beauty's sake alone. By investing in beautiful landscaping, we become co-creators with the God of beauty. But beautifying the church grounds is also a form of welcome and outreach. I even look upon it as a specialized ministry. The messages that attractive landscaping sends out are that something is happening at this church and these people appreciate real beauty. But perhaps most important of all, beautifying the church grounds causes people to stop and take notice of a place they may have blindly passed by for months or years.

But beautifying the church grounds is not limited to flowers and shrubs. The parking lot may need to be sealed and striped. The trees may need to be trimmed so passersby can see the building. The children's playground equipment (if any) may need to be painted or replaced altogether. And the wood surfaces of the building may need to be scraped and repainted. A church I know of recently celebrated a major anniversary (a milestone in years of service). I must give them credit for designing and erecting a big vinyl banner, which they displayed in front of their building celebrating and announcing their milestone. But I could not help but notice that all the while the paint on their front door (which was next to their banner!) was faded and peeling, making it look as though no one really cared about the looks of their building. *How sad,* I thought to myself every time I passed by that church, *that while celebrating such a milestone in ministry no one put forth the effort to spend $10 on a can of paint to liven up the front door!*

A good idea is to appoint four or five people to do a "walk-through" of your church grounds and facilities as though they were first-time, critical visitors, while jotting down all the areas where some beautifying and improvements would make a tremendous difference.

✳TIP:

Beauty causes people to take notice of your church.

13

Door Hangers

DOOR HANGERS CAN BE A UNIQUE AND NONTHREATENING WAY TO get church members involved in outreach who are too shy or self-conscious to actually speak to their neighbors about visiting church. Some very attractive and thought-provoking hangers may be secured from some denominational offices or services such as Church Ad Resources. I prefer to use the hangers that bear a message the church wants to get across but that also have a space for the local congregation's personalized message. The church's name, location, telephone number, e-mail address, and website should be included in the space provided.

In my previous parish we hung approximately fifteen hundred of our denomination's door hangers on the front doors in the neighborhood immediately around our church. The percentage of return is not high, I must admit, although we have had a few families come and join from the streets where the hangers were placed. But one of the most rewarding aspects of seeking volunteers to distribute the hangers is getting new members excited and involved in the ministry of hospitality and welcome.

❋TIP:
*Door hangers can be a nonthreatening form
of welcome and outreach.*

14

Cable Television Service Ads

SOME CABLE COMPANIES HAVE A STATION WHERE COMMUNITY NEWS bulletins run twenty-four hours a day, seven days a week, free of charge. This is done as a community service. Others may charge a nominal fee for running a church ad for so many days. Several years ago, when we were getting ready to launch a new church, we ran an ad with the cable television community news channel to advertise our first worship service. In recent years we have used the community channel to advertise our fall Harvest Festival and Dinner. Granted, not everyone sits all day watching the community news channel, but the idea is to get the name of your church before the community in as many ways as possible. Cable television ads are just another way of doing that.

An added benefit is that when you let your church members know that their church has an ad running on cable television, it instills a sense of pride.

*TIP:
Contact your local cable television provider.

15

Ad in Yellow Pages

MOST OF US, WHEN WE GO TO THE YELLOW PAGES TO LOOK FOR A hardware store, cab company, computer repair center, or some other such business, are immediately attracted to the large, well-designed ads. Why should it be any different with churches? Yet, one of the best, but perhaps often overlooked, forms of community advertisement is the Yellow Pages. A recent scanning of the Albany, New York, Yellow Pages churches listing revealed that of six full pages of church listings for the extended Capital Region (some six hundred listings in all), less than one-half dozen churches had invested in any sort of ad in addition to their small, two or three line listing. If we want to get the attention of new arrivals in our community and other people who have decided to start looking for a church, why not consider investing some well-spent advertising dollars on a quality Yellow Page ad?

*TIP:
Check out your Yellow Pages.

16

Positive Answering
Machine Message

AFTER FINDING A CHURCH'S NAME IN THE YELLOW PAGES, MANY people will call the church office to inquire about service times and other programs. If no one is available around the clock to receive such telephone calls, the church needs to have a positive, upbeat, informative, inviting message that will make people want to visit your church. Personally, I think it is good, generally speaking, for the message to be recorded by the minister. The message should include the church's name, a short statement that alludes to the church's slogan or mission statement, the street location, service times, and an invitation to leave a message—which will be promptly followed up on. A sample message might sound like this: "Hello, you have reached First Church. No matter who you are or where you are on life's journey, you are welcome here. We are located at 101 Any Street. Worship is at 10:30 a.m., and Spiritual Formation for all ages is at 9:30 a.m. on Sundays. Please leave a message after the tone, and we will return your call as soon as possible. And we will look forward to seeing you this Sunday."

✳TIP:

The church needs to have a positive answering machine message.

Attractive, Up-to-date Website

THE WORLD IS GOING HIGH-TECH. AND SO MUST THE CHURCH IF IT is to keep up. Some experts contend that the way that younger adults decide upon a church to visit is by surfing the Internet and finding a church that appears to be what they are looking for.

A church website may include a picture of the church, the pastor's name, the church's purpose or mission statement, service times, small group opportunities (including meeting times), missions supported by the church, denominational affiliation, the church's strengths that should serve to attract newcomers, a brief history, and the like. It might also include links to other denominational or religious websites.

In almost every congregation there should be at least one computer savvy person who can work with the pastor or someone else in the congregation to design an attractive, eye-catching website that will make people want to visit. And the more interactive the site, I am told, the better.

✳TIP:
To attract the younger generations,
we must go high-tech and build an attractive website.

18

Brochures

A CHURCH'S BROCHURE—WHICH MAY SERVE AS THE PRIMARY defining piece of the church's ministry, mission, purpose, program offerings, and so on—should be designed with care. It should be positive but truthful in the information it shares, but it should not contain much in the way of doctrine. People may want to know a church's basic beliefs or defining concept, but most are not interested in heavy dogma. People are more interested in what the church has to offer by way of programs and how the church carries out its mission in the world. Brochures can be made available to all first-time visitors and others who express an interest in the church. They can be distributed in the community, passed out at community fairs, or mailed to all residents on certain streets or zip codes.

If possible, the brochure should be printed in color and include pictures (with permission secured and granted) of different activities and faces from the congregation.

⁎TIP:

The publicity brochure may serve
as the congregation's primary tool of welcome.

Mass Mailings

By using bulk mailings aimed at certain zip codes or receiving mailing labels listing new residents who move into your area from companies that provide such services, you can get your message out to a lot of people with very little effort. Another option is to purchase a Crisscross Street index that gives names of residents according to street names, set up a database of residents within a certain radius of your church, and send them publicity materials. Organizations such as the Church Ad Project offer some catchy and thought-provoking materials that can be customized to include your church's name and other pertinent information. For mass mailings to be effective they must be top-notch, state-of-the-art pieces, and they must be utilized more than once. Experts say it takes at least three mass mailings to the same household to get attention. So a church might consider sending one mailing a week for a number of weeks, or one a month for a number of months, or one at special seasons of the year such as Advent, Christmas, Lent, and Easter.

✻TIP:
*Mass mailings get the church's name
out in the community on a mass scale.*

20

Thirty Special Sundays per Year

SEVERAL YEARS AGO, LYLE E. SCHALLER NOTED THE OBVIOUS: THAT people like to come to church for special events and programs. When children present a play or skit during worship, when mothers are recognized on Mother's Day, when loved ones who have passed on are remembered on Memorial Day or All Saints Sunday, more people come. So the more special Sundays a congregation can plan per year the greater the annual average attendance will be. But, more importantly, when something special is going on at your church, the members will be more inclined to invite unchurched friends, relatives, neighbors, and coworkers. Some of those invited will come and, hopefully, some of them will like what they see and hear and come again. So at the beginning of the year (January or new church school year) the church leadership would do well to sit down, go over the calendar, and brainstorm about how many special Sundays can be planned for the next twelve months. Then the key is to advertise sufficiently the "coming attractions" so as to generate interest and support.

✴TIP:
How many special Sundays can your church plan for next year?

21

Supporting It All with Prayer

ALL THAT IS DONE SHOULD BE SUPPORTED WITH PRAYER. I LIKE RICK Warren's suggestion in his book *The Purpose Driven Church* that the prayer we should be praying as church leaders is not, "Lord, bless what we are doing," but rather, "Lord, help us to do what you are blessing." That is, we need to be open to the Spirit's moving among us and plan our programs, outreach, and means of welcome accordingly. Many of the programs and ideas that worked forty years ago when the American church was at its heyday are no longer viable. We live in a different time, a day when God is doing a new thing. Prayer helps us discern where God is leading us.

One of the most important small group opportunities that a church can begin is a prayer circle or meditation group for those who feel a passion for prayer or have an interest in spiritual meditation (every pastor can probably name a few members for whom prayer or meditation is very important). The circle or group might meet weekly, every other week, or once a month to study together some classic work on prayer or meditation, share community needs, and then spend some time praying or meditating together for the needs that are expressed. Each meeting can include a focus on the hospitality and welcome ministry of the church.

✳**TIP:**
*All our plans and activities should be supported
by prayer and meditation.*

QUESTIONS FOR DISCUSSION AND ACTION

1. What are three things your church could do to make your church building and grounds more attractive to newcomers?

_____

_____

_____

2. What is one thing your church could do to attract attention?

_____

_____

_____

3. What is the one overarching purpose of your church?

_____

_____

_____

4. Can you name one thing your church could do to encourage members to invite their friends, relatives, neighbors, and coworkers to church?

_____

_____

_____

5. What are some special, "less threatening" church events that might be planned as a way to invite and welcome newcomers?

_____

_____

_____

ITEMS IN PART ONE THAT NEED ATTENTION

You may want to check off the following items as they are accomplished at your church:

____ Understanding your purpose

____ Writing a purpose statement

____ Personal invitation—word of mouth

____ Friend Day

____ Newspaper ads/articles

____ Newspaper flyers/inserts

____ Community visitation

____ Telephoning

____ Special programs and events

____ Outdoor banners

____ Attractive signage

____ Beautifying church and grounds—paint, plant flowers and shrubs, etc.

____ Door hangers

____ Cable television service ads

____ Phonebook yellow pages ad

____ Positive message on answering machine stating service times

____ Attractive, up-to-date website

____ Distributing brochures

____ Mass mailings

____ Planning as many special Sundays per year as possible

____ Supporting it all with prayer or focused meditation

PART TWO

Making People Feel Welcome

Do not neglect to show
hospitality to strangers, for by
doing that some have entertained
angels without knowing it.

HEBREWS 13:2

22

Visitor and Handicap Parking

ONE OF THE MOST DIFFICULT ACCOMPLISHMENTS IN MANY CHURCHES may be getting long-time members to see with visitor sympathetic eyes. This becomes apparent when blocking off the best parking spaces in the lot for newcomers is mentioned. In one rural church I served we voted to pave and line the church parking lot. Having known nothing but a graveled parking lot, which was prone to being gullied by heavy rains, this, of course, made all of the members proud. However, marking off the best spots nearest to the door for handicapped persons did not go over so well with one member in particular. "Gary," as I will call him, had had the practice for years of arriving early on Sunday morning and parking directly in front of the church, the spot closest to the building. When we decided to mark that spot off for handicapped parking, the next Sunday Gary came to church as usual, but he did not stay. He left in a huff, angry that we had taken "his" parking spot.

In retrospect, I see that the situation could have been handled differently. I, or one of the church elders, could have gone to Gary beforehand and asked him if he would consider "giving up his parking spot" for handicapped worshipers. Approached in this way, he might have been inclined to do so gracefully, having a say in the matter. But no one expected Gary to react so strongly. However, there is a happy ending. After staying away a few weeks, Gary made his way back and all was forgiven and forgotten.

In another church it was a constant struggle to keep our regular, healthy members from parking in handicap and even first-time visitor spots, just because they were unwilling to walk a few extra steps.

The point is, marking off and truly reserving special spots for handicapped worshipers and first-time visitors should be handled carefully. However, it should be done. Nothing can be more negative than a handicapped worshiper or first-time visitor coming to church and being unable to find a suitable place to park. Having a ready spot available says, "You are welcome here. We were expecting you."

※ **TIP:**

Having special parking spots for handicapped worshipers and first-time visitors says, "We were expecting you."

Signs to Direct Newcomers

JUST AS IMPORTANT AS SPECIAL PARKING SPOTS FOR HANDICAPPED worshipers and visitors are appropriate, easy-to-see, easy-to-read signs that direct people into the building, as well as direct them once they have found their way in. Wandering aimlessly through an unfamiliar church building, especially if it is large, without knowing where you are going can be an intimidating experience for most of us, but even more so for those who have little or no previous church experience. Signs that direct first-timers to the sanctuary, church office, nursery, restrooms, fellowship hall, and so forth are essential.

※ **TIP:**

Adequate signage helps newcomers feel more at ease.

24

Handicap Accessible Facilities

Any new buildings that are constructed these days of necessity are handicap accessible. However, there are probably a lot of older buildings that are still inaccessible to those in wheelchairs or others who have other physical limitations. Of all institutions on earth, the church should be the most inclusive and open to all. Handicap ramps, elevators or lifts, wide doorways to accommodate wheelchairs, handicap accessible restroom facilities—these are just a few of the features that churches seeking to be inclusive and to grow should consider if they are not already in place.

But sensitive churches may also think about adding features for the sight and hearing impaired, such as Braille on doors, persons to sign during services, or hearing devices in the pews.

TIP:
Of all places, the church should be
the most inclusive and accessible to all.

Enthusiastic Greeters

IF A CHURCH WANTS TO WELCOME NEW MEMBERS, THEN IT SHOULD take very seriously the idea of stationing friendly, inviting greeters at strategic locations to welcome newcomers. These persons should be handpicked and trained in the art of greeting. Ideally they would be in addition to the ushers who pass out worship programs. Depending on the size of the church building and property, a number of greeters might be stationed at different places so as to direct newcomers—in the parking lot, on the front steps, in the hallways, just outside the sanctuary, and any other strategic locations. Greeters should exhibit a smile but not be overly jovial or too familiar with worshipers. They should be warm and inviting, but not intimidating. They should be helpful in giving directions, but not nosy. The right greeter can make newcomers feel at ease and glad to be with you, but the wrong greeter can easily frighten newcomers away. We want the newcomers' first impression to be positive.

✱TIP:
*Friendly, inviting greeters should be
strategically stationed.*

26

Clean, State-of-the-art Classrooms

TODAY THERE IS NO EXCUSE FOR DARK, DRAB, MUSTY CLASSROOMS that look as though they have not been remodeled since the 1960s. Yet, I fear, in too many church buildings this is the case. Curtains falling off the wall, scaling paint, inappropriate tables and chairs, outdated posters, and the like need to go to make room for a more contemporary look and modern technology. Paint or wallpaper should be brightened up. Tables and chairs need to be modern and age- and size-appropriate (no toddlers sitting on adult chairs at tall, eight-foot tables). Today's church classrooms might include a computer for every child to access biblical materials. The lesson plan might include a video or DVD clip, or laptop computer and projector that incorporate a power point presentation or nature images or religious artwork that complements the lesson. The possibilities are endless. The point is, we should not expect our church school students— whether they are children or adults—to live in a high-tech world and then come to church on Sunday and be thrown back into the 1960s.

⁕TIP:
Classrooms should be state-of-the-art.

27

Top-notch Nursery and Quality Childcare

THE NICEST ROOM IN ANY CHURCH BUILDING COULD ARGUABLY BE the nursery. When families with young children go shopping for a church, their decision very well may be decided by the attractiveness and cleanliness, or lack thereof, of the nursery facilities. As we inspect our church nurseries, what do we find there? Old, broken-down furniture? Dirty, castaway toys? Out-of-date curtains and wall hangings?

Fresh, bright paint; a new, clean floor; nice, age-appropriate furniture and toys; perhaps even some colorful Bible story murals on the walls—these are things that we should strive for in creating a suitable nursery not only for first-time visitors but for the children who already go there as well. If a church is faced with the decision of remodeling the nursery or the kitchen, it should most definitely go with the nursery first. Then, as young families join, the remodeling of the kitchen can follow.

✳TIP:
The nursery should be the nicest room in the church.

28

Properly Welcoming Newcomers

During our "Ritual of Fellowship" time in the worship hour, I have the practice of saying, "We extend a special welcome to those who are worshiping with us for the first time today." Notice that I did not say "We welcome those who are *visiting* with us today." And I also do not ask visitors, or first-time worshipers, to stand and introduce themselves. People want to know that their presence matters and that someone takes notice, but most people do not like to be singled out and asked to stand in a crowd of strange people and introduce themselves. (Regarding getting the names of newcomers, I address that in a following section.) After the service, as people file from the sanctuary to the fellowship hall for coffee hour, I greet first-time worshipers by saying something like, "Good morning! It's great to see you this morning. Can you join us for coffee hour?" I then trust our greeters or members of our Hospitality Team to make sure the first-timers find their place at the coffee bar and are made to feel welcome during that time of fellowship.

✳TIP:
*It is important to properly welcome visitors
in a way that doesn't cause embarrassment.*

29

Positive, Uplifting, Expectant Worship

FOR MOST NEWCOMERS TO A CHURCH, THE ENTRY POINT WILL BE THE Sunday morning (or for those churches that are willing to experiment with some other time of the week, such as Saturday evening) worship hour. Most people don't walk into the worship service of a strange church by chance. They are looking for something. A personal or family crisis has ensued. They have recently begun searching spiritually. Some event like September 11, the Southeast Asia tsunami, or Hurricane Katrina has caused them to think about the ultimate matters of life. They have started a family. What people are often looking for when visiting a new church is a positive, uplifting, expectant worship service that offers them hope.

This presents a real challenge for the conscientious preparers and leaders of worship. No longer can a minister, music director, or other leader of worship run into church thirty minutes prior to the service and select the hymns, a call to worship, and responsive reading from the church's hymnal (I have actually seen this happen on a number of occasions). Planning and preparing for worship requires time and forethought that should start far—days, weeks, perhaps even months—in advance of the service. From the opening welcome to the call to worship to the readings (and how they are read), hymns, prayers, and other pieces of the liturgy to the benediction—all should be chosen and integrated in such a way that the service is uplifting to all and imparts a sense of hope.

✳TIP:

People come to a new church looking for hope.

30

Enabling Worshipers to Sense the Sacred

CLOSELY RELATED TO THE PRECEDING SUGGESTION IS STRIVING TO enable worshipers to get a sense of the presence of the Sacred or the Divine. The Divine, the Holy, the Great Mystery—call God what you will, most people come to worship in search of "Holy ground." When they leave, they want to know deep down that they have been in the presence of the Divine. Sometimes I feel in this regard that those of us who are responsible for planning and leading worship are like the blind trying to lead the blind, because the presence and activity of the Divine cannot be orchestrated. We cannot just bring God out of the box on Sunday morning or command God to appear at will like a genie in a bottle.

Yet, we can begin worship preparations with a prayer that the Sacred will guide and enable us to prepare an inspiring, uplifting worship experience in which God's divine presence can be known. We can pour over the biblical texts, making them a part of us. We can study a variety of possible hymns and liturgical resources, looking for pieces that speak to us. If we hear the voice of the Holy and feel the presence of the Divine in a certain hymn or liturgical selection, then just maybe others will too.

Furthermore, those who lead the worship can pray for the blessing and presence of God in their leadership. They can pray that all the fruits of the Spirit as Paul enumerates them—love, joy, peace, patience, kindness, generosity, faithfulness, gentleness, and self-control (Gal. 5:22–23)—will be manifest within them. Hopefully and prayerfully, we will have prepared ourselves and the service in such a way that people can leave saying, as did Jacob, "Surely the Lord is in this place" (Gen. 28:16).

✳TIP:

Worshipers long for a sense of the presence of the Sacred.

31

Ritual of Fellowship

RITUALS OF FELLOWSHIP VARY FROM CHURCH TO CHURCH, BUT MY suggestion is that at some point in the service, worshipers be issued the invitation to turn and greet all those around them, "as we pass the peace one with another." This is a good way for first-time worshipers to be greeted and welcomed again (hopefully they have already been warmly greeted upon entering), as well as a good time for old-timers to greet those they haven't seen in awhile. In one congregation I served, people get up from their seats and consciously move toward others across the aisle or even across the sanctuary. It is not uncommon for a few members of the choir to leave the choir loft to greet people on the sanctuary floor. This practice only takes a couple of minutes, but it holds great meaning for long-time members and first-time worshipers alike.

✳TIP:
*The ritual of fellowship is a good way
to help newcomers relax and feel welcomed.*

Verbal Instructions for Newcomers

FOR PERSONS WHO HAVE VERY LITTLE EXPERIENCE IN ATTENDING church, the worship service can be quite intimidating. And for that reason some subtle verbal instructions from the pastor or other worship leader are in order. For instance, some people will not know the proper times to stand or be seated. The leader may be sensitive to newcomers who may hesitate and spare them embarrassment by saying, "Will those who are able please stand" or "You may be seated." Instructions about which hymnal to use, or where to find the scripture reading, or whether to hold the communion elements "so all may eat together"—these are just a few of the ways that we can be sensitive to newcomers in our midst and help make them more at ease.

✳TIP:
The sensitive worship leader aims
to help newcomers feel at ease.

33

Newcomer-friendly Worship Bulletin

THE WORSHIP PROGRAM SHOULD ALSO BE NEWCOMER FRIENDLY. IT should be easy to read, and not in an ancient type font just because someone thinks it looks "churchy." The words of all prayers such as the Lord's Prayer, and all responses such as the Doxology or Gloria Patri, should be printed in the worship program itself, or there should be instructions as to where the words may be easily found. The point is, it should not be taken for granted that everyone who comes will automatically know the Lord's Prayer or Doxology.

Yet, I have seen this to be the case in too many a worship experience. There should be no uncertainty or cause for embarrassment in the worship experience, if at all possible. Perhaps everything should be printed in the worship program as though this was the first time for everyone to be present at such an occasion.

❋TIP:
*The worship bulletin should be clear and concise
so all worshipers will know what to do and say.*

34

Celebrative and Colorful Banners

NOT ONLY CAN OUTDOOR BANNERS BE EYE-CATCHING AND WELL worth what it costs to hang them, but indoor banners can pay big dividends and convey hospitality as well. Colorful and well-crafted felt or quilted seasonal banners draw attention and stir interest. They make worship more enjoyable and meaningful. Special mission-related banners can have an even greater impact, as they are unexpected. Some make banners depicting Third World outreach, while others design banners about justice issues. Regardless, banners say something. They say this church is doing something. This church is making a statement. The message presented in a visual and aesthetic medium becomes a powerful message that connects with people.

The possibilities for worship banners are endless. The liturgical seasons of the year (Advent, Christmas, Epiphany, Lent, Easter, Pentecost), the special holidays (Thanksgiving, Unity Sunday, Valentine's Day, Mother's Day, Father's Day, All Saints Day), and special celebrations and anniversaries all cry out to be noted in artistic ways. We are spiritually and religiously moved by visual images and the arts as much as or more than we are by the spoken word. The creation of banners can be achieved by any number of small groups in the church. Or a church could plan a "banner day" as an intergenerational event, bringing together young and old alike to create a number of banners for the coming year.

*TIP:

Colorful banners make worship more meaningful.

35

Offering Excellent Service Music

THIS, I REALIZE, MAY BE A TOUCHY SUBJECT, ESPECIALLY FOR SMALL churches that must depend on a volunteer musician, possibly whomever can be roped into doing the job. But nothing kills the spirit of a worship service faster than a slow, dragging hymn littered with sour notes. If at all possible, churches that seek to grow should revitalize their music ministry. The best musician available should be secured. The instrument should be kept in tune. The pace of the music should be uplifting. Many years ago when my family and I were working with a new church development and meeting in a daycare center, my wife said to me,, "You should never have ended the service with that song. The service should have ended on an upbeat, positive note." She was right. The words of the hymn I had chosen for that day had gone well with the sermon's theme. But the tune was somewhat like a funeral dirge.

This brings me to my next point: care should be taken in the selection of hymns, not only for musical considerations, but also for the words and message you want to convey. There are a number of staple hymns that I grew up on and used to love that I can no longer in good conscience let myself sing. With the proliferation of Christian hymnody, praise songs, and choruses, the possibilities are mind-boggling, regardless of where one falls on the theological spectrum. On the shelf in my study are at least ten or twelve hymnals. I try to draw from a variety of sources throughout the year, utilizing both familiar traditional hymns as well as newer, contemporary ones. It behooves today's worship leaders to look far and wide for music that will be true to their churches, the message they want to proclaim, and at the same time speak to those of the current generation.

❋TIP:

The quality of a church's music can make or break it.

36

Attractive, Up-to-date Bulletin Boards

THE BULLETIN BOARD CAN BECOME THE INFORMATION CENTER OF A church that not only keeps its regular members informed, but also acquaints newcomers with the church, its programs, and its many activities. The bulletin board can become an outreach tool that acquaints newcomers with your church's ministry and mission.

The board can hold pictures of church events. It can include letters of gratitude from places where support has been rendered. It can include photos of members actively involved in mission or in the world. And it can connect the local congregation to the denomination or wider church. Nothing is more of a turnoff than an unattractive, outdated, cluttered bulletin board. On the other hand, nothing can be more eye-catching than an attractive bulletin board that portrays the true personality of an active, serving congregation.

✳**TIP:**
The bulletin board can become an outreach tool
that acquaints newcomers with your
church's ministry and mission

37

Coffee/Fellowship Time

ONE OF THE BEST MEANS OF ASSIMILATING NEWCOMERS, I HAVE found, is the coffee/fellowship time following the worship service. Such a time of fellowship has been a regular part of our Sunday for the past sixteen years. There are, however, some important pointers that I would like to share.

First, someone should be trained to lead newcomers to the table. "Can you join us for coffee? If so, I can show you the way." Newcomers might thus be encouraged to attend so they do not head out the door as soon as the benediction is given.

Second, space should be made for newcomers at the coffee bar. Regular members should be sensitive to newcomers, being courteous and letting them know they are important, rather than crowding around the coffee bar in such a way as to make it difficult for newcomers to work their way in (I have seen this happen).

Third, once in the fellowship area, newcomers should never be allowed to sit or stand alone. In addition to greeters or others who are trained to welcome newcomers, the entire congregation should become sensitive to newcomers and scan the room to see who might need some company. Too often the long-time members are so preoccupied with catching up with old friends that they forget the stranger in their midst. Let us not forget, as the writer of Hebrews cautions, "to show hospitality to strangers, for by doing that some have entertained angels without knowing it" (Heb. 13:2).

✳**TIP:**

One of the best ways to assimilate newcomers
is during the coffee/fellowship time following worship.

Providing Genuine, Loving Community

PEOPLE ARE LOOKING FOR COMMUNITY—GENUINE, LOVING community—and nurturing relationships. This is what we must seek to provide. No easy Steps 1, 2, 3 can be given for providing such community. It is difficult, complex work that takes years in the making. Nevertheless, it is something toward which every church should be striving. Regardless of where one's church falls on the theological spectrum or what the denominational affiliation, what people are looking for most of all is loving community. A church may be "theologically correct" and "doctrinally sound" in every way. But if it does not display loving community, it might as well be playing a noisy gong or clanging cymbal (1 Cor. 13:1).

✳TIP:
People are looking for genuine, loving community.

QUESTIONS FOR DISCUSSION AND ACTION

1. For someone who has no previous church involvement and is visiting your church for the first time, what part of the worship service would make him or her feel uncomfortable or lost?

_____

_____

_____

2. What direction signs to assist newcomers are most needed on your church property or inside your building?

_____

_____

3. Which is the nicest classroom in your educational space? The least nice and in need of the most attention?

_____

_____

4. What method does your church have of encouraging those present to greet each other on Sunday morning? Is it adequate?

_____

_____

_____

5. In what ways could your church improve its bulletin board so as to make it a tool for outreach?

_____

_____

_____

ITEMS IN PART TWO THAT NEED ATTENTION

You may want to check off the following items as they are accomplished at your church:

_____ Visitor and handicap parking

_____ Appropriate signs to direct newcomers—childcare, sanctuary, restrooms, etc.

_____ Handicap accessible building and worship space

_____ Enthusiastic greeters

_____ Clean, state-of-the-art classrooms

_____ Top-notch nursery and quality childcare

_____ Welcoming (but not embarrassing) newcomers

_____ Positive, uplifting, expectant worship service that offers hope

_____ Enabling worshipers to get a sense of the presence of God

_____ Ritual of fellowship

_____ Verbal instructions in the worship service for newcomers

_____ Newcomer friendly worship bulletin—easy to read, printed prayers, hymn numbers

_____ Celebrative and colorful banners

_____ Excellent service music

_____ Attractive, up-to-date bulletin boards with pictures and missions information

_____ Coffee/fellowship time following the service— lead newcomers to the table

_____ Providing genuine, loving community and nurturing relationships

PART THREE

Seeing People Return

*Dear friend, when you extend
hospitality to Christian brothers and
sisters, even when they are strangers,
you make the faith visible.*

3 JOHN 5 (The Message)

39

Worship Service That Offers Hope (Again!)

IF FIRST-TIME WORSHIPERS ARE TO COME AGAIN, MOST LIKELY THEY will have received something from the worship service that on some level spoke to their need. If they leave with a sense of hope, they may be inclined to come again in search of more hope for a different problem on a different day. If they heard a positive word to help them live a better life, they may come back for another positive word. If they experienced loving community, they may return and seek to become a part of that loving community.

So let it be said again that the entry point for most people to a new church is the weekly worship hour. Making it a positive, uplifting, hope-filled hour cannot be overstressed.

✳TIP:
If newcomers leave uplifted and with a sense of hope,
they will likely come again.

Practical, Interest-piquing Messages

GONE, IN MY OPINION, ARE THE DAYS OF DOCTRINAL AND THEO-logical sermons that debate the insignificant issues of faith. People are looking for practical messages that are directly applicable to their daily lives. They are looking for messages that include a picture of human struggle, that answer real-life faith questions, that emphasize good news, and that offer hope. But this does not mean that sermons have to be shallow or theologically poor in their content. To prepare and present quality sermons that also remain true to the sacred texts or traditions presents a challenge to any preacher in today's world. But it is a challenge that must be taken seriously. Though all the pressure for a church's success or failure cannot be put upon the pastor by any means, as it takes everyone working together to make a welcoming church, there is a certain amount of pressure on the pastor as preacher and probably as worship leader to offer the best that can be offered. Nothing in this regard will substitute for hard work and dedication in worship planning and sermon preparation.

❋TIP:
*The pastor as preacher plays
a role in church revitalization.*

41

Registration Pads

As PEOPLE BEGIN TO AGAIN TAKE THEIR SEATS DURING THE "RITUAL of Fellowship" (see tip 31 in part 2), they may be asked to pick up the registration book that is on the end of their pew or row and "please note your presence and pass it on so others may do likewise." Notice that I did not say, "Please *sign* the registration book." A lot of people are hesitant to sign anything. Signing says making a commitment. Noting their presence is less threatening.

Also, it is important that longtime members note their presence on the registration book as well, even if they have been coming fifty years. Newcomers will be more inclined to give their name and address if they see others beside them do the same. The ushers or someone else designated for such a task should collect the registration sheets so they can be used for follow-up on Monday morning and then the names entered into a database for future mailings (more about this to come).

✳**TIP:**
*Encourage first-time worshipers to note
their presence in a registration book or pad.*

42

Connecting Newcomers with Others

IN ORDER FOR NEWCOMERS TO BECOME ACTIVELY INVOLVED IN AND unite with a new church, most often they need to establish friendships. Though some people will attend and possibly join a church as "loners," most people are looking to establish meaningful friendships. Church growth experts tell us that most people who fail to establish friendships in a new church will not stay. So not only can the reader focus on befriending newcomers, but it is also important that newcomers be introduced to others in the congregation with similar backgrounds, interests, occupations, and hobbies.

Introducing newcomers to others in the congregation who have like interests presents another exciting possibility, that of starting new small groups that become not only meaningful entry points for newcomers but places where spiritual care and opportunities for mission can occur as well. For instance, at our previous church we were able to introduce some newcomers to a few others in the congregation who have an interest in quilting. Those introductions led to the formation of the Quilting Circle, which led to new friendships being established, which led to small group care and concern, which led to a mission project. The Quilting Circle learned that the local hospital needed a new memorial quilt for the birthing wing. When parents suffer the loss of a child through miscarriage or stillbirth, the child's name is written on the quilt as a living remembrance of the child who was lost but is not forgotten. At a Sunday morning worship service the chaplain of the hospital was present to receive the quilt from the Quilting Circle. That moment was a moving experience for everyone. A couple of weeks later, the quilt was even shown on the local television channel as a part of the story about the hospital's ministry to families who lose their infant children. It all came about because persons with like interests were introduced.

✻TIP:
*Most newcomers need to establish
meaningful friendships.*

Brief Follow-up Visit by the Laity

IF POSSIBLE, WITHIN FORTY-EIGHT HOURS OF THE WORSHIP SERVICE a layperson may want to pay a serendipitous visit to first-time worshipers. This visit should take place at the front door and last no longer than three to five minutes. The visitor can obtain the name and address of first-time worshipers from the pastor, greeters, or church office. A suitable time (perhaps mid-afternoon on Sunday or between 6–8 P.M. on Monday or Tuesday evening) should be chosen. The visitor should knock on the door, step back away from the door, and put a smile on his or face. When the person comes to the door, the layperson can say something like this: "Hello, my name is John Smith, and I am a member of First Church. We just wanted to let you know how happy we are that you joined us for worship, and I wanted to see if you had any questions about our church that I might answer." At this point the person being visited should direct the conversation. If questions are asked, they should be answered as truthfully as possible. If there are none, then the visitor might say, "Well, we have a hospitality gift for you for being with us, and we do hope you will come again." (See the next tip.) The visitor should leave in as gracious a manner as possible so that it was a positive experience. Such a visit lets the newcomers know that someone noticed and the church is genuine about hoping to see them again.

✳TIP:
Follow-up visits let first-time worshipers know the church cares.

Hospitality Gift

ACCOMPANYING THE FOLLOW-UP VISIT SHOULD BE SOME SORT OF hospitality gift. Hospitality gifts help newcomers remember the church and its warm hospitality. Our congregation had beautiful porcelain coffee mugs printed for a small cost with the church's picture and information on them. We prepare them by placing one of the pastor's calling cards, a church ink pen, and a pack of cocoa mix in them, and then wrap them in clear cellophane and tie a ribbon around the top. Some churches bake homemade bread, pies, or cookies to take to newcomers. The idea is to convey hospitality, friendliness, and the assurance that "we're glad you came and hope you will come again."

✳TIP:
Hospitality gifts help newcomers remember the church and its warm hospitality.

45

Letter or Handwritten Note

IF ADDRESSES OF NEWCOMERS ARE LISTED, THE PASTOR SHOULD WRITE a personal note or send a letter (for me it varies depending on the person) on Monday morning. In this note or letter I try to let the newcomers know that we are glad they chose to worship with us, list some of the positive things I feel our church has to offer, extend an offer to meet with them if they desire to ask any questions about the church, extend an offer to assist them in any way that they might need, and close with an assurance of our hope that we will see them again soon. Along with this letter I include one of my calling cards and a copy of our church's brochure.

TIP:
A note or letter from the pastor
should go out on Monday morning.

Phone Call from the Pastor

AFTER A FEW DAYS HAVE PASSED, PERHAPS LONG ENOUGH FOR THE newcomers to receive their note in the mail, or certainly after the newcomers' second visit, the pastor should follow up with a quick telephone call to let them know that their presence was noted and important and to see if there are any questions about the church that the pastor might answer. I generally say something like this: "Hello, this is Pastor Hammer at First Church. Am I calling at an inconvenient time? Good. I just wanted to follow up on the note I had sent you and tell you again how good it is to have you with us in worship, and I wanted to see if there are any questions I might answer or any way that I might assist you." Over the years a lot of persons I have called have seemed impressed that the pastor took enough time to call them. The conversation should be brief, upbeat, and positive, and the close of the conversation gracious. Hopefully a door will be opened for more in-depth conversation in the future.

❋TIP:
Newcomers may be impressed
that the pastor took time to call.

Encouraging Small Group Involvement

THE TWO MOST IMPORTANT ASPECTS OF CHURCH LIFE ARE CELEBRATIVE corporate worship and small group involvement. One of the church's goals should be to encourage newcomers to get involved in one of the church's many (hopefully) small group opportunities. I have found that choir is an excellent entry point into active church life. But our previous congregation also saw success in adult church school classes, a Young Adult Professionals & Students (YAPS) group, quilting circle, exercise group, book discussion group, and fourth Friday movie night, in addition to the traditional Sunday morning religious education time. The point is, just as newcomers need to make friends that will help keep them connected, they also need to become involved in a small group where friendships can be established and spirituality and discipleship can be nurtured.

❋TIP:
*Newcomers need to become involved
in a small group where spiritual care can occur.*

48

Sending the Church Newsletter

NEWCOMERS WHO ARE WILLING TO GIVE THEIR NAME AND ADDRESS should be added to the church's newsletter mailing list and kept on that list for at least six months or so. Occasionally persons who are church shopping will visit and then be absent for a number of months only to return after they have determined yours is the church they were looking for after all. So a small amount of postage and printing costs is a small price to pay when taking into account those newcomers who are sent the church newsletter and other appropriate publications and who may eventually become full members.

TIP:

*Newcomers should be added
to the church's newsletter mailing list.*

Utilizing an
Online Midweek Message

ONE OF THE EASIEST YET MOST EFFECTIVE WAYS THAT PASTORS AND churches can connect with newcomers, as well stay connected with their regular members, is through what I call a "Midweek Message." I am amazed that all pastors are not doing this. Each Wednesday I send a one-page or less online message to all members who have e-mail and any friends who request it. In that message I announce the upcoming Sunday's sermon title and try to pique interest in the topic. I also announce any special events that may be taking place or special plans that may be included in the worship service. I often give a one- or two-line quotation from the previous Sunday's sermon for those who missed it, a positive thought for the week, and a brief prayer for the week. The response has been very positive. People know what is going on, and via the miracle of the Internet, busy people still feel connected with the pastor. Such things as an online midweek message (and website as well) are positive draws especially for today's younger generation for whom technology is so important.

✳TIP:
The Internet is a good way to make a connection
with members and newcomers.

50

Assisting Newcomers in Exercising Their Gifts

NEWCOMERS WILL NEED TO GET INVOLVED IN THE MINISTRY AND programs of the church in some way for them to feel and stay connected. But this *does not* necessarily mean putting them on a boring committee! Rather, newcomers need to be assisted in finding their place of service according to their interests, talents, and what the Apostle Paul calls the "gifts of the Spirit." There are any number of resources for assisting members in discovering and nurturing their spiritual gifts. One I have used with some adaptation is produced by the Christian Reformed Church (it is somewhat theologically conservative, but can be adapted). When members—newcomers and long-time members alike—discover and find ways to utilize their gifts, great things can happen. People tend to come to life and get excited about their faith. Ministry and service suddenly start to make sense in a tangible way. And the church is apt to experience revitalization.

✳ TIP:
Discovering their spiritual gifts helps people stay connected.

51

Living the Law of Love

FOR A CHURCH OR OTHER COMMUNITY OF FAITH TO REALLY CONVEY a sense of welcome and hospitality, they must let the world know that they are seeking to live the law of love (see Matt. 22:37–39). And it cannot be false or just for show. It must be genuine; it must be real. Living the supreme law of love will influence everything we do in the church setting. It will affect the way we relate to one another in committee meetings, the way we speak (or don't speak) about one another in private conversations, the way we minister to one another in times of crisis such as hospitalization and death, and the way we rejoice with another during those times of celebration such as baptism and marriage.

❋TIP:
*The welcoming, growing community
must live the law of love.*

Staying True to
Your Purpose Statement

AS STATED IN THE BEGINNING OF THIS BOOK, THE PURPOSE STATEMENT can serve as a "polar star" that guides a church in all that it does. Newcomers who start to a church do so, in part at least, because they like the church's purpose statement and are assured that the church is staying true to that stated purpose. A church posting and publicizing a beautiful purpose statement that does not fit its actual programs and ministries might be compared to someone who would put a beautiful Cadillac emblem on the front of an old, beat-up Ford. It obviously would be out of place. So congregations do well to examine everything they are doing and everything they plan to do in the future and measure their worthiness against the purpose statement that has been adopted. When a church has a worthy purpose statement that is true to its sacred texts and traditions, true to what the church has been called to do, and true to a church's unique identity and personality, and when a church is true to that purpose statement, then hopefully it will experience revitalization and growth.

✳TIP:

Each church should to its own self be true.

QUESTIONS FOR DISCUSSION AND ACTION

1. What is one good way to attract young adults to your church?

_____

_____

_____

2. Who in your church is appointed to help connect newcomers with others in the congregation?

_____

_____

_____

3. What type of hospitality gift would work best to give to first-time worshipers in your community?

_____

_____

_____

4. What means are available in your church for encouraging small group involvement?

_____

_____

_____

5. What approach is being used to assist newcomers in discovering, nurturing, and utilizing their natural and spiritual gifts?

_____

_____

_____

ITEMS IN PART THREE THAT NEED ATTENTION

You may want to check off the following items as they are accomplished at your church:

_____ Positive, uplifting worship service that offers hope (again!)

_____ Practical, interest-piquing sermons

_____ Registration pads—ask all worshipers to please note their presence

_____ Connecting newcomers with others in the congregation

_____ Brief follow-up visit by lay volunteers

_____ Hospitality gift

_____ Personally signed note or letter from the pastor

_____ Phone call from the pastor

_____ Encouraging small group involvement

_____ Sending the church newsletter

_____ Utilizing an online weekly message

_____ Assisting newcomers in exercising their spiritual gifts

_____ Living the law of love

_____ Staying true to the church's purpose statement

APPENDIX A

Illustrations of Selected Resources

ILLUSTRATION FOR CHAPTER 4, "FRIEND DAY"

You are invited to

Friend Day

a celebration of friendship

to be held at

FIRST CONGREGATIONAL CHURCH
UNITED CHURCH OF CHRIST

405 Quail Street
Albany, NY 12208
Sunday, March 5, 2006
At 10:30 A.M.

A special coffee hour will follow at 11:30 A.M.

ILLUSTRATION FOR CHAPTER 5, "NEWSPAPER ADS AND ARTICLES"

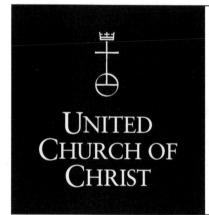

FIRST
CONGREGATIONAL
CHURCH

United Church of Christ
405 Quail Street
Albany, New York 12208

www.firstcongregationalalbany.org
518-482-4580
Worship ■ 10:30 A.M.
Christmas Eve Service ■ 6:30 P.M.

God is still speaking.

ILLUSTRATION FOR CHAPTER 6, "NEWSPAPER FLYERS (INSERTS)"

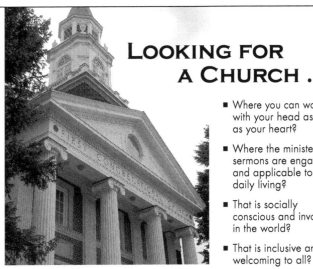

LOOKING FOR
A CHURCH . . .

- Where you can worship with your head as well as your heart?

- Where the minister's sermons are engaging and applicable to daily living?

- That is socially conscious and involved in the world?

- That is inclusive and welcoming to all?

- That has a quality music program and restored 100-year-old pipe organ?

- That offers a beautiful sanctuary conducive to meditation?

WHY NOT
CONSIDER
VISITING

FIRST CONGREGATIONAL CHURCH
UNITED CHURCH OF CHRIST

Located at 405 Quail Street
1 block north of New Scotland Avenue
www.firstcongregationalalbany.org
518-482-4580 ▪ 1stCong@nycap.rr.com
Sunday Worship 10:30 A.M.
Christian Education 9:45 A.M.

ILLUSTRATION FOR CHAPTER 11, "ATTRACTIVE SIGNAGE"

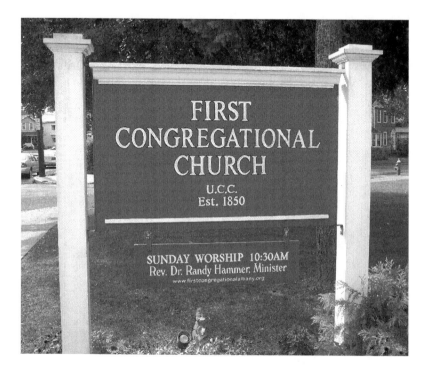

ILLUSTRATION FOR CHAPTER 20, "THIRTY SPECIAL SUNDAYS PER YEAR"

Many church growth experts agree that the more "special Sundays" a church can plan, the greater the attendance, and hence, the greater the membership. Here are some examples:

MONTH	CALENDAR EVENT	SPECIAL SUNDAY ACTIVITIES
SEPTEMBER	Welcome back & rally Sunday	Introduce SS, material, teachers
	Membership Sunday	Celebrate membership
OCTOBER	World Communion	Communion/unity
	Harvest Festival Recognition	Awards to workers/celebration
	Trick or Trunk	Goodies for kids
NOVEMBER	Friend Day	Invite friends/special coffee hour
	Pilgrim/Thanksgiving	Pilgrim attire/service of thanks
DECEMBER	Advent	Ways to celebrate Advent in home
	Children's pageant	Children's play and dinner
	Christmas Sunday service	Christmas emphasis
	Christmas Eve service	Lessons and carols
JANUARY	New Year	Emphasize new beginnings
	Epiphany	"Here come the kings"
	Diversity Sunday	African American music
	Souper Bowl Sunday	Children's skit
FEBRUARY	Valentine's Sunday	Hearts/candy for all
	First Sunday in Lent	Purple attire Sunday
MARCH	Blanket Sunday	Children's skit
	St. Patrick's Sunday	Green attire Sunday
APRIL	Palm Sunday	Distribute palms
	Easter Sunday	Breakfast and egg hunt
MAY	Fifty-year member recognition	Silver tea
	Mother's Day	Flowers for mothers
	Annual Meeting	Dinner
	Memorial Sunday	Remember loved ones
	Pentecost Sunday	Red attire day/balloons/cake
JUNE	Children's Day	Program and picnic
	Father's Day	Recognize fathers
JULY	Independence Sunday	Celebration of religious freedom
AUGUST	Nature Sunday	God in nature

ILLUSTRATION FOR CHAPTER 25, "ENTHUSIASTIC GREETERS"

Checklist for Greeters

1. Plan to arrive at least ten minutes prior to the start of the service and be ready to greet all worshipers, noting especially newcomers, at the entrance(s) to the sanctuary.

2. Wear a smile and be courteous and friendly to all worshipers.

3. Introduce yourself to newcomers.

4. If possible, secure, remember, write down, and pass on to the pastor the names of first-time worshipers.

5. During the "Passing the Peace" or "Ritual of Fellowship" time in the worship service, make sure that newcomers are greeted and welcomed.

6. At the close of the worship service, take the initiative in inviting newcomers to the coffee/fellowship time. Show them the way, and lead them to the coffee/food bar.

7. During the coffee/fellowship time, make sure no newcomers are left standing or sitting alone. *This is very important!*

8. Make meaningful connections between newcomers with other members of the congregation. For instance, if you learn that a newcomer is a teacher or musician, you might introduce him or her to another teacher or musician in the congregation.

9. Share with newcomers dates and times of other meetings and services that might be of interest to them, such as movie nights, quilting circle, Christian education, book discussion group, choir, and so on.

10. Be sensitive to any special needs or areas of concern (one of the primary reasons that many people first decide to start to church is personal need or a crisis in their lives).

11. As newcomers prepare to leave, again tell them how happy we were to have them and let them know you hope they will come again.

12. Share any information that you gain with the pastor.

ILLUSTRATION FOR CHAPTER 29, "POSITIVE, UPLIFTING, EXPECTANT WORSHIP"

Tips for Enhanced Scripture Reading

1. Read your assigned passage(s) ALOUD a number of times prior to the service.

2. Practice reading your passage(s) slowly and meditatively, so that you enter into the spirit and meaning of the passage(s).

3. Pay attention to pauses, change in speakers, changes in tone, and so on, and try to reflect these as you read.

4. Check the proper pronunciation of words with which you are unfamiliar. A self-pronouncing Bible helps tremendously.

5. The more you prepare, the more confident you will feel.

6. On the day of actual reading, be careful to read loud enough so all may hear, and at an appropriate speed—not too fast, but also not too slow.

7. You may introduce your reading(s) with "Our first reading today is from the book of [name book]"; and "our second reading is from the book of [name book]" or "from Psalm [give psalm number]."

8. In readings from the Psalms, the word "Selah" should not be read aloud. "Selah" was a musical term in ancient Israel. Also, when reading from a psalm, the proper introduction is "Our first reading today is from Psalm Whatever," not "Psalms Whatever" (singular, not plural).

9. Remember that the reading of scripture should be the most dignified element in the worship service.

10. If you have questions about pronunciation or other matters related to your reading(s), feel free to ask the pastor. Thank you!

ILLUSTRATION FOR CHAPTER 44, "HOSPITALITY GIFT"

ILLUSTRATION FOR CHAPTER 45, "LETTER OR HANDWRITTEN NOTE"

FIRST CONGREGATIONAL UNITED CHURCH OF CHRIST
405 Quail Street
Albany, New York 12208

Tele: 518.482.4580 Fax: 518.438.7945

Organized in 1850
*Celebrating over 150
years of returning the
favor of God's love.*

March 2, 2009

Anyone
Main Street
Anytown, USA

Dear Anyone:

Again I want to tell you how happy we are that you joined us for worship. We sincerely hope that you felt comfortable and were blessed in some way by the service. We try to make our services uplifting and the sermons applicable to daily living.

We believe that First Congregational Church has some good things to offer those who are seeking a new church home:

- A number of opportunities for small group involvement, fellowship, and spiritual growth, including children and adult Christian education, GROW Focus Group, exercise group, quilting circle, choir, Young Adult & Professional Fellowship, 4th Friday Movie Night, and our coffee hour
- Friendly, loving people
- An inclusive fellowship that is open and welcoming to all
- A progressive theology
- A beautiful church building and sanctuary
- A good music program
- A mind for missions in the community and the world
- A caring fellowship that seeks to stay in touch with the people

I would be most happy to visit with you in your home, my office, or perhaps at a coffee shop to answer any questions you might have about our church beliefs or programs, if or when you are so inclined.

Thanks again for choosing to worship with us and for your interest in our church. If we can serve you in any way, please feel free to call me.

Sincerely,

Rev. Randy Hammer

APPENDIX B

Bulletin Inserts

The following articles are intended to be used as inserts in bulletins. Taken from "There You Grow," copyright 2006 by Randy Hammer, they may be copied for congregational use, but not reproduced or sold for profit.

A BULLETIN ON CHURCH HOSPITALITY AND OUTREACH
by Rev. Dr. Randy Hammer

WHERE ARE YOU GOING TO PARK?

Having visited a few of the growing, contemporary churches here and there across the country, we have found that they tend to reserve the best spots closest to the building for handicapped members and first-time worshipers. The truth is, it is hard enough for people to get up the nerve to go to an unfamiliar church for the first time. It takes courage to pull into the parking lot, get out of the car, and walk into a strange (unfamiliar) building. Having reserved spots says, "Welcome. We are expecting you. We are glad you are here. We want to make coming here as easy and pleasant as possible."

However, it has been my experience in previous pastorates that having such spots can be a tremendous temptation for the rest of the membership. In one church, we even had one healthy member get upset because we marked off the best spot, closest to the building, as a handicap spot. Everyone should have known that that was HIS spot and he had parked there for years!

So parking lot etiquette is an area where everyone can help. As tempting as it might be to park in the blue handicap spots, healthy members should refrain from doing so. Of course, if they have a handicap tag, then they ought to. And even though it might be convenient to whip into (especially if you are running a few minutes late) a visitor's spot, we should reconsider, find another spot, and walk the few extra steps.

Being the church of the "extravagant welcome," to employ a phrase coined by the Rev. John Thomas, president and general minister of the United Church of Christ, means being mindful of the smallest of details, right down to where we park our cars.

A BULLETIN ON CHURCH HOSPITALITY AND OUTREACH
by Rev. Dr. Randy Hammer

NOT FOR MEMBERS ONLY

Have you ever felt a real, spiritual need to go to church, perhaps a new church, but when you got there the door was locked?

Pastor and author Anthony B. Robinson tells of going to visit a church one Sunday morning when he was free from pastoral responsibilities. He parked on a near side street and walked to the front door of the church. He put his hand on the handle and pulled, but it would not open. The door was locked tight. It was time for the Sunday service to begin, but he could not get in. He knocked on the door and waited. After a while, an older member of the congregation pushed the door open and invited him in, saying, "We usually don't open this door; everyone knows to come in through the back door." Robinson observes, "Well, this arrangement was very cozy and friendly if you were part of the 'everyone' who made up the aging and shrinking cohort of the congregation. If not, you hardly felt welcomed. The message was clear: members only. The congregation's members were oblivious to the message of the locked front door as well as to the implications of their confidence that 'everyone knows to come in through the back door.'"

The "locked door" that Robinson speaks of can be both literal and figurative. Certainly it is important that the front doors of our church are unlocked when it is time for services to begin. But "locked doors" are many and varied and can be any challenge or hindrance that first-time worshipers encounter from the second they pull into our parking lot and until the moment when they get in their car to leave. Such things as not knowing which door to enter, no one to greet or welcome them when they arrive, being uncomfortable with an unfamiliar service of worship, not knowing what to do when it is time to "Pass the Peace," not feeling comfortable walking up to the coffee bar, or feeling alone during fellowship hour can be "locked doors" that make people feel that a church is for members only. All of us do well to put ourselves in the place of a first-time worshiper and be mindful of never letting anyone encounter a "locked door" or feel like our church is for members only.

A BULLETIN ON CHURCH HOSPITALITY AND OUTREACH
by Rev. Dr. Randy Hammer

FRIEND DAY

Some eighteen thousand people were once surveyed by Church Growth, Inc., to determine how they became involved in the church. Surprisingly, over 70 percent responded that they became involved in a particular church because of the influence of friends and/or relatives. If a congregation is not growing, then one main reason may be that its members are not inviting.

Yet, many people find it hard to speak to their friends and relatives about coming to church. That is where "Friend Day" comes in. "Friend Day" is a special Sunday set aside for all members to invite their Friends, Relatives, Acquaintances, Neighbors, and Co-workers or Club members (FRANC) to church. It is a day to celebrate friendship as well as to acquaint those we love who may not now be involved in a church with what our church has to offer. Some members will invite their friends on "Friend Day" when they will no other time. Such a special day gives them the excuse to do so. And some people will come on "Friend Day" who will come no other time, if for no other reason than they are doing a favor for their friend, who happens to be a member of your church.

We believe that we have something special to share, a positive, inclusive message that many in our community are hungering to hear. But most of them will never know about it because they do not know that our church even exists.

For "Friend Day" to work, it must be planned and publicized well in advance and mentioned often from the pulpit, in the worship bulletin, church newsletter, and so on. Invitations and envelopes should be made available so that all members need to do is sign the invitation and address and stamp the envelope and drop it in the mail.

Just think: if every member brought one other person on "Friend Day," not only would attendance double on that day, but think of how many new people would discover the church of the extravagant welcome and radical hospitality.

A BULLETIN ON CHURCH HOSPITALITY AND OUTREACH
by Rev. Dr. Randy Hammer

A PLACE WHERE *ALL* ARE WELCOME?

It was Palm Sunday 2005. Excitement was in the air. Palm leaves adorned the chancel. The "Hosanna" banner was hung. Attendance was above average. It was time for the festive music to begin.

At 10:28 A.M., I was standing in the narthex of First Congregational Church donning robe and stole as is customary in our congregation. The organist had already begun to play the Prelude. It was time for me to process up the aisle and take my place on the platform for the opening hymn. And then it happened.

In the front doors walked two men. I could not believe my eyes! One of them was carrying a giant, yellow tabby cat. We were well into the "God Is Still Speaking," "No matter who you are or where you are on life's journey, you are welcome here" campaign. What should I do?

As "Darryl" (not his real name) walked up the steps to the sanctuary with cat in tow, I glanced over at our head usher, who was at the opposite side of the narthex, and quickly searched my mind for words that would be appropriate. "Hi, I'm Darryl," the man said excitedly. The strong odor of alcohol struck me in the face the moment he opened his mouth.

"Good morning, Darryl," I replied, with outstretched hand. "We are glad to see you this morning. However, we usually do not have cats in church," I said as politely as possible.

"Oh, I know that, but he was following me down the street and I didn't have time to take him back, and I couldn't just leave him outside. And I *have* to be in church today."

"I understand," I assured him, "but if your cat gets loose during the service, it could cause quite a disturbance" I replied, again as politely as possible.

"Oh, he won't get loose; I'll hold onto him tight." And with that Darryl bolted into the sanctuary with his friend right behind him and they took a seat near the front, about three pews from the pulpit and communion table. Soon after the service began, the friend's cell phone rang, and he leisurely got up and left the service while talking to the person on the other end, leaving Darryl and his cat alone.

Well, as soon as the pipe organ bellowed the opening hymn, the cat became very unhappy and started clawing his way up Darryl's chest and shoulders, frantically trying to escape. The cat started crying as cats in distress often do. As soon as the cat would claw his way up Darryl's arms, chest, and shoulders until it looked as though he would climb right down the back of the pew and escape, Darryl would drag him down again.

One of our members went and found a cardboard box and gave it to Darryl to house the cat, but the cat would have none of that so the box sat empty on the pew.

When it came time for cares and concerns to be voiced, Darryl jumped to his feet and said, "My name is Darryl, and I'm an alcoholic and I will be joining First Congregational Church. I'll be going to rehab soon, and I want you all to pray for me."

As I looked out across the congregation and listened to the cat cry, growl, and hiss, I could see the uneasy look on many faces. But no one really knew what to do under the circumstances. Somehow I managed to make it through the service, pretending that the cat's presence was nothing out of the ordinary.

At the close of the service, many of our members made a point to be friendly to Darryl, and to his cat as well. After everyone had left, one of our ushers took it upon himself to clean the massive balls of cat hair from the pew cushion and the blood (yes, blood from Darryl's arms) from the back of the pew.

Darryl returned about three times and was welcomed every time he came. Then he went off to rehab and we lost touch with him, in spite of my repeated attempts to contact him.

We have often wondered if God, by sending Darryl and his giant cat to us, was testing us to see if we really meant what we had been saying: "No matter who you are or where you are on life's journey, you are welcome here." Nowhere is it written that extravagant hospitality is easy. But it has been written to be careful about welcoming strangers, because some have entertained angels without knowing it.

A BULLETIN ON CHURCH HOSPITALITY AND OUTREACH
by Rev. Dr. Randy Hammer

GETTING READY FOR COMPANY

B efore one puts a house on the market and opens it up to the first showing, a lot of work usually needs to be done—touch-up painting, caulking, trimming shrubs and trees, carpet cleaning, and so forth. In other words, there are a lot of preparations to get one's house ready for company.

It is no different in the church. As we take steps for renewed hospitality and growth, we need to first make sure we are ready for company. We want our church facilities to look absolutely the best before company arrives. Getting ready for company is something all of us need to be conscious of and involved in.

For instance, as first-time visitors dropping off infants at our nursery, what would you see? Does the room emit a sense of welcome, warmth, cleanliness, and, above all, safety? Some church growth experts contend that of all spaces in a church facility the nursery should be the nicest and most state-of-the-art.

What about the entrance area? Is it warm and welcoming? Or is it cluttered and dusty? Do our facilities say that people who "live" here care about the upkeep and appearance? We need to train ourselves to see our church building and grounds as first-time visitors might see them. A good idea is to secure three or four persons, perhaps most recent additions to the congregation, or even better, friends or relatives of congregation members, to do a "first-time visitor" walk-through of the building, noting how they see the building as a first-time visitor sees it.

If we were expecting special first-time visitors to come to our homes for a couple of hours, most of us would feel the need to do some straightening up. It should be no different in the church if we expect to be welcome hosts.

A BULLETIN ON CHURCH HOSPITALITY AND OUTREACH
by Rev. Dr. Randy Hammer

ANYTHING TO BE LEARNED FROM MEGACHURCHES?

The so-called "megachurches," congregations averaging two thousand or more in worship each weekend, receive a lot of criticism: They must not be true to the gospel and are making it too easy for people to become members; that is why they are growing. And growing rapidly they are indeed. There are now more than 1,200 megachurches in America, and indications are that the number will continue to grow. They are here to stay.

But could it be that megachurches are doing at least *some things* right, which helps contribute to their growth? And are we willing to admit that we might actually learn something from them?

What got me to thinking about all this is a report recently released by the Hartford Institute for Religion and Research and Leadership Network (see http://www.leadnet.org/links/Megachurches Today2005). The Institute identified 1,210 Protestant megachurches in America, then surveyed, studied, and tabulated responses from many of them. Some of the findings indicate that in many cases they are doing things right and that many of the myths surrounding them are false.

As I studied the findings, I found the following five points about megachurches to be particularly relevant for all churches, mega, medium-sized, or small, and whether they are conservative, moderate, or liberal.

- Worship services are filled with a sense of God's presence, are inspirational, joyful, and thought-provoking.
- Megachurches are willing to attempt and embrace change; this leads to growth.
- Megachurches (91 percent anyway) have a clear mission and purpose.
- The rate of growth is strongly correlated with the absence of conflict in the congregation.
- "Megachurches grow because excited attendees tell their friends."

A BULLETIN ON CHURCH HOSPITALITY AND OUTREACH
by Rev. Dr. Randy Hammer

RESPONDING TO THE CURRENT REVOLUTION

The culture of the church is changing. It is so much different than it was thirty years ago when I began preparing for ministry. But since changes in the church occur slowly over time, we may not be attuned to them.

Christian pollster and futurist George Barna has written a book titled *Revolution*, in which he talks about the revolution or tremendous changes that are taking place in the American church. Barna states that the percentage of Americans for whom the local congregation is their primary avenue of expressing their faith is falling. In other words, more and more people are finding the local church to be irrelevant, or more and more people are deciding that they can be Christian outside the established church or organized religion. Barna contends that the best Christians are not always found in churches. In other words, people who truly live the principles of Christ (for instance, as taught in the Sermon on the Mount in Matthew 5–7) and who are performing Christ's mission in the world are not always involved in local churches. Sometimes one will see a "better Christian" *outside* the church than within.

The fastest growing Christian groups in America today are the house church and Internet churches. This trend has significant ramifications for local churches, including ours. With church affiliation falling off, being a part of a *growing* congregation will become more and more difficult.

Barna observes that local churches and their leaders can choose to ignore this revolution taking place in American Christianity, or they can have their eyes open and seek to respond accordingly. It seems to me that this revolution says two things to us: (1) it behooves us to be truly Christian in our speech, character, and the overall way we live our lives (we should be anyway) as a positive witness to the world; and (2) we should be about finding more ways to carry out Christ's mission in the world so that when others see how we live and serve, they will be drawn to us and want to express their faith in covenant with us.

A BULLETIN ON CHURCH HOSPITALITY AND OUTREACH
by Rev. Dr. Randy Hammer

BEING A MISSIONAL CHURCH

In his book *Inside the Organic Church: Learning from 12 Emerging Congregations* Bob Whitesel reports on an in-depth study of more than forty of the so-called emerging churches that are popping up around the world. These are churches largely made up of younger (twenties- to thirties-aged) members who are breaking out of traditional paradigms to do church in a different way. There is a wealth of good information in the book that can be appreciated by any church—traditional, emerging, or otherwise.

Hence, being schooled in church growth literature, I was happy to read (p. xviii) that one of the pastors the author quotes states, "Church growth needs to be recovered. Not in its bizarre fringe forms, but in its simplicity and straightforwardness that helps churches grow." But as I am always quick to note, church growth is not to be seen as an end in itself. We do not seek growth for growth's sake alone. We seek to grow so we can better perform our mission in the community and world.

This leads me to another observation in the book, what it means to be missional. Whitesel states, "Being 'missional' simply means to be outward and others-focused with the goals of expressing and sharing the love of Jesus. The church was not created for itself to remain inward-focused, but actually created to worship God and to spread [God's] love to others. . . . Therefore, we don't have a 'missions department' because the whole church is a mission" (p. 44). This quote was from Pastor Dan Kimball of the Vintage Faith emerging church in Santa Cruz, California.

The spiritual maturity of a congregation often can be determined by ascertaining what it believes about its purpose and how it understands and describes its mission. We do not assemble week after week just so we can be made to feel good about ourselves (although going to worship does make us feel good, doesn't it?). Rather, a much greater purpose in assembling is that we can better understand and be better equipped—collectively and individually—to fulfill our God-given mission in the world.

A BULLETIN ON CHURCH HOSPITALITY AND OUTREACH
by Rev. Dr. Randy Hammer

LEARNING FROM THE EMERGING CHURCH

There is a lot that we in the traditional church can learn from the so-called emerging church (or organic church, depending on who you are reading). Emerging church is a broad term signifying the many new churches that are springing up around the world that do not fit into the traditional church mold. These are churches that appeal to the postmodern, post-Christian generation, persons who might not attend church otherwise.

And there is not *one* emerging church model, but rather hundreds, perhaps thousands, of different forms the emerging church is taking. Yet there are some common characteristics to the new emerging churches. One of them is heavy reliance upon artwork and the visual in worship. They are incorporating a variety of artistic elements in their worship services in order to enhance worshipers' experience with God or the Sacred. The form that such artistic elements might take range from having an art table where participants might paint a picture or mold something from clay in the course of the service, to carefully arranged artistic focal points in the worship space that complement the theme of the day, to projecting slides of nature or ancient religious artwork on the wall to complement the sermon, to a patterned arrangement of burning candles, or any number of other things.

It should not be surprising that another characteristic of the emerging church is emphasis on experience rather than rationalism and logic. Pains are taken to enable worshipers to *experience* the Sacred with all of the senses as opposed to just *talking about* the Sacred by way of a lecture-type sermon.

Some of us already have dabbled in incorporating more artistic and visual elements in worship through such means as seasonal banners, the Advent wreath, a nativity scene, and so on. And we include the visual every time we baptize or celebrate the Eucharist.

So what is wrong with setting up a small artistic worship focal point for other seasons of the year such as Lent, Easter, and Pentecost that would complement and reinforce the seasonal theme or weekly messages? That way people are spoken to and moved not only by what they hear, but also by what they see, and perhaps by what they might touch, smell, or even taste.

If the church hopes to continue to be vital and relevant for a new generation, we need to learn to adapt and keep up with the times. If we can learn something from the emerging church movement, then God bless us.

To learn more about the emerging church, check out *The Emerging Church* by Dan Kimball, *Inside the Organic Church* by Bob Whitesel, or the website www.vintagefaith.com.

A BULLETIN ON CHURCH HOSPITALITY AND OUTREACH
by Rev. Dr. Randy Hammer

WHY PEOPLE VISIT NEW CHURCHES AND RETURN

There is an interesting new book on evangelism in mainline churches titled *Unbinding the Gospel: Real Life Evangelism.* The work is the result of a four-year study of 150 churches and interviews with more than a thousand people, funded by the Lilly Endowment. Just two of the important questions that the author, Martha Grace Reese, addresses are pertinent to every congregation that is seeking to reach out and experience growth: (1) Why do people first visit the church they join? and (2) What gets visitors back for the second, third, and fourth visits?

The answers didn't surprise me in the least. They are the same answers I have been finding for years in evangelism and church growth materials. Regarding why people first visit the church they join, "Almost 60% of new members of evangelistic churches get there first because a person invited them, or because they know someone in the church" (p. 76). The author hits the proverbial nail on the head when she says, "the one most effective thing you can do to get evangelism going in your church is to invite people to church!" (p. 76).

Regarding why people return, "38% of new Christians and 30% of new members with a church background . . . say they return repeatedly because of the warmth, the love, the 'realness' of the church members" (p. 77). The percentage of those who returned because of the pastor? Only 14 percent.

The author concludes, "So, an invitation seems to get these visitors there in the first place, but the welcome, warmth, and authenticity of people [followed by] the personality, teaching, and preaching of the pastor and worship bring visitors *back* to experience church life again" (p. 77).

The evidence is indisputable: whether or not a church grows or continues to grow primarily rests with its members. It takes both aspects for growth to occur—everyone inviting friends, relatives, neighbors, and coworkers to worship and other church activities, and then everyone demonstrating genuine warmth, welcome, and love to all who enter.

A BULLETIN ON CHURCH HOSPITALITY AND OUTREACH
by Rev. Dr. Randy Hammer

LEARNING TO LISTEN

In *Beyond Church Growth: Action Plans for Developing a Dynamic Church,* Robert E. Logan states, "The successful church of the twenty-first century and beyond will be one that learns how to listen to people, establishes a culturally relevant philosophy of ministry, and adapts its ministry strategies to their ever-changing needs" (p. 74). That is a mouthful. And it is a challenge to say the least.

The need to learn how to listen is a recurring theme we keep seeing as we study trends in today's churches. Ministry is becoming more about holy listening and less about so much speaking from the perspective that we have all the answers.

What we in the church need to be about more than ever is learning to listen to one another. The author of the New Testament book of James put it well when he (most likely a he) wrote: "You must understand this, my beloved: let everyone be quick to listen, slow to speak, slow to anger" (1:19).

Newer members need to listen to those who have been around a long time in order to get a sense of the congregation's history and heritage. And members who have been around a long time need to listen to newer members who come with new ideas and fresh ways of looking at things. Just because a church has done the same thing for fifty years doesn't mean it is still the right or best thing to be doing.

And then there is the need to listen to what new friends and neighbors might have to say to us about what they are looking for in a church home and what it is about the traditional church that turns them off.

But in a broader sense, learning to listen to one another and trying to see things from the perspective of others without getting angry or defensive is part of what being Christian is all about. Too often we may be tempted to jump to conclusions and prejudge another, whereas if we had only taken time to listen we might understand and see things much differently. Learning to listen is growing together in Christian love.

A BULLETIN ON CHURCH HOSPITALITY AND OUTREACH
by Rev. Dr. Randy Hammer

CELEBRATING MEMBERSHIP

On the first Sunday of May, First Congregational Church, United Church of Christ, of Albany, New York, hosts their annual Silver Tea for those persons who have been members of First Congregational Church for fifty years or longer. On that day during a special coffee hour the membership expresses appreciation for these saints of God.

And appreciation should be shown. Being a member of the same congregation for fifty years or more is a rare thing in this day and time. The transitory nature of our society where a large portion of the population moves every few years, the decline of the volunteering and joining mentality, and the practice of "church shopping" in search of the place that best meets one's needs all serve to work against long-term commitment and membership. So such commitment and dedication are worthy of celebration.

Fifty-year members have a lot of stories to tell and wisdom to share. It is imperative that those stories and wisdom be passed on to younger generations. We need to be listening to what long-time members have to say, taking their pictures, and recording the history about the church that should be saved for posterity.

As congregations who are serious about a revitalization program, we know that in order to plot where we are going it is important to know where we have been. We want to build on the successes and avoid the pitfalls of those times that were not so successful. All churches have both in their history.

We need to talk with long-time members and gain from them all the insights that can be gained. We should congratulate them and express a word of appreciation for their part in supporting the church in years past, the church that we all know and love. It is important that we are mindful of the fact that were it not for the sacrifices and service of those who have gone before, the church we know and love would not be here today.

A BULLETIN ON CHURCH HOSPITALITY AND OUTREACH
by Rev. Dr. Randy Hammer

THE IMPORTANCE OF CARING

In a speech delivered at the University of Connecticut Health Center's 2007 graduation exercises, one of the graduates shared a quotation worth remembering and passing along. Speaking to those who had just received degrees in dentistry and medicine, the graduate observed, "People are much more interested in knowing how much you care before they care how much you know." When it comes to healing, feeling listened to and cared for is an important part of the equation. How incisive! And how true it is, not only for doctors and dentists ready to go forth and practice their healing arts, but for ministers as well.

But could not the same thing also be said of churches? When newcomers enter our doors in search of a new church home, they may be much more interested in knowing how much we care before they care about how much we know about a particular creed or doctrine. Doctrinal differences and arguments—over how many angels can dance on the head of a pin, or whether or not predestination is a biblical doctrine, or the precise nature of the Trinity, and so on—may have mattered in bygone centuries. Battles were waged and people were burned at the stake over such questions. But by and large such issues are no longer as important as they once were.

What many people are looking for today in a church home is a sense of community: a place of caring and belonging where people actually live out Jesus' example and teachings on true love and compassion. In spite of—perhaps because of—technological advances such as the Internet, e-mail, and instant messaging, people feel isolated and long to experience genuine community. Technology, instant messaging, Internet religion, or television church will never take the place of the local church and the sense of community and personal caring that it can provide.

So, as we fellowship and as we welcome newcomers who regularly pass through our doors, let us show each other as well as newcomers how much we really care.

A BULLETIN ON CHURCH HOSPITALITY AND OUTREACH
by Rev. Dr. Randy Hammer

ON THE SAFE SIDE

A certain pastor had just arrived at an ancient Coptic monastery out in the desert, nearly a day's journey from Cairo, Egypt. He was astonished at the welcome he received. The monks treated the pastor as if he were the one and only important guest they had been awaiting since the place was established in the twelfth century. They served a fine meal, showed him to a comfortable room, and brought him a bouquet of fresh flowers. The pastor was then greeted by the abbot of the monastery, Father Jeremiah. "Wow!" exclaimed the pastor. "You sure know how to treat visitors."

Father Jeremiah replied, "We always treat guests as if they were angels, just to be on the safe side."

Herb Miller tells this story in *How to Build a Magnetic Church* pointing out how important it is for churches to convey a friendly, hospitable atmosphere to newcomers.

The reason for the monks' hospitable nature was based, no doubt, on the verse in the Christian scriptures that says, "Do not neglect to show hospitality to strangers, for by doing that some have entertained angels without knowing it" (Heb. 13:2).

Think about it: What if all of us always went out of our way to be kind and hospitable to strangers? What if we treated everyone like we would treat an angel? How might the world be different? How might our lives be blessed? How many new friends might we make?

An angel from God need not be a winged, heavenly creature. Sometimes in the scriptures angels are nothing more than humans sent by God on a special mission to bless people's lives. They come bearing a message, or bringing good news.

Who knows how many newcomers will pass through the doors of our church? Some of them will feel led to make our congregation their church home. Some will become close friends. Some (if not all) of them might just be "angels" sent by God to bring good news, fresh ideas, and much-needed gifts and talents. How important it is that we welcome every one as we would welcome an angel, "just to be on the safe side."

A BULLETIN ON CHURCH HOSPITALITY AND OUTREACH
by Rev. Dr. Randy Hammer

PROVIDING OPPORTUNITIES FOR CONNECTION

In a recent article published by the Alban Institute, Carol Howard Merrit focuses on young adults and why they come to church. Merritt states, "When a young person walks into a church, it's a significant moment. . . . [S]he enters the church looking for something. She searches for connection in her displacement: connection with God through spiritual practices, connection with her neighbors through an intergenerational community, and connection with the world through social justice outreach." I think there is a lot of truth in what Merrit has to say. She has put her finger on three all-important components of church involvement, regardless of one's age or stage of life—connection with God, connection via community, and connection through social justice outreach. How important it is for churches to make sure that all three opportunities are available.

Connection with God comes through such avenues as meaningful worship, Christian education classes, spiritual formation opportunities, book discussion groups, prayer circles, and the like.

Connection via community is provided through the Sunday coffee/fellowship time, fellowship dinners, small group gatherings, quilting circles, men's and women's fellowships, youth groups, and so on.

Connection through social justice outreach can come by working on a Habitat for Humanity House, serving at the rescue mission or Interfaith Partnership for the Homeless, assisting at a local food bank, or contributing to any number of special annual offerings that help make for a more just, peaceful world and make a positive difference in persons' lives.

These things listed are far beyond what any pastor of any church can provide. It requires many minds and hearts to make sure that all three of these important connections are in ample supply. Together members of a congregation can brainstorm and plan so as to make sure that these important connections are available, not just for young adults who enter the church doors, but for all who come looking for connection with God, community, and social justice outreach.

A BULLETIN ON CHURCH HOSPITALITY AND OUTREACH
by Rev. Dr. Randy Hammer

THE FRIENDSHIP FACTOR

How much of a role does the "friendship factor" play in persons deciding to pay a first-time visit to a new church and in their decision to return, get involved, and ultimately join? Probably much more than we might initially think.

Martha Grace Reese, in her book titled *Unbinding the Gospel: Real Life Evangelism*, states that almost 60 percent of people first visit a new church because someone invited them or they know someone in that church. This is consistent with other statistics I have read.

Furthermore, church revitalization experts contend that before newcomers can really feel at home in a church they must have made some friends there. Oftentimes such friendships can form because of similar ages or particular interests, such as astronomy, computers, music, quilting, snow skiing, even theological discussion groups. People look forward to coming to church in part because they know they are going to find some friends there who know their names and who also look forward to seeing and spending time with them.

So, as we think about how the church can continue to grow in the ministry of hospitality and welcome, we do well to think about ways all of us can promote the "friendship factor" in our congregation. We can go out of our way to make friends with newcomers. We can make sure that no one is sitting or standing alone during the coffee/fellowship time. We can invite newcomers of like ages or with similar interests to our homes for coffee or a meal. We can invite newcomers to small group meetings. When we learn of a personal or family need that someone might have, we can do what we can to be a friendly support.

As we become more intentional about promoting and nurturing new friendships in our congregation, we not only move closer toward becoming the church that God calls us to be. But we also see the fruits of our efforts in the continued growth of our congregation and the growth of talents and individual resources that new members bring with them.

A BULLETIN ON CHURCH HOSPITALITY AND OUTREACH
by Rev. Dr. Randy Hammer

NEW PERSPECTIVES ON EVANGELISM

While driving across the state of Virginia recently, I got behind a car that had one of those personalized license plates. The plate read IN2GZUS. It may take a moment to figure it out. But once you do, you realize that the driver of that car must have been an ardent Christian. And this was her (I think the driver was a young woman) way of doing evangelism.

As we drive across this great land of ours we can see a variety of such evangelistic efforts, if we have our eyes open to see them. Bumper stickers that say, "I'm a Jesus fan." Billboards that warn, "Prepare to Meet Thy God." Bridge graffiti that reads, "Trust Jesus." Flashing church signs that ask, "Are You Ready for the Judgment?" The ways that Christians seek to do "evangelism" are many and varied.

But there are other, less in-your-face methods of practicing real-life evangelism. Evangelism at heart is nothing more than sharing the good news of the blessings we have received from God, which most often come through the church we all have come to know and love. Evangelism is loving one another as God has loved us. It is extending extravagant hospitality to all who come through our doors in search of a word of hope and loving community. Many of us may have already been practicing evangelism, but we just haven't labeled it as such. And many more could become "evangelists" by sharing a positive word of how God has blessed us, by more concerted efforts to show love to newcomers, and by sharing a smile and hand of welcome to first-time worshipers.

The season of Pentecost is the season of evangelism. It is the season for all of us to think more seriously about being evangelists—sharers of good news and extenders of hospitality.

(Just don't go running to the DMV to order your IN2GZUS license plate. That one's already taken.)

BRIEF ANNOTATED BIBLIOGRAPHY

GENERAL CHURCH GROWTH AND DEVELOPMENT RESOURCES

Bass, Diana Butler. *Christianity for the Rest of Us.* New York: HarperOne, 2006. A study of flourishing mainline progressive to liberal churches and identification of the common characteristics that have led to their revitalization and growth. An invaluable resource.

Callahan, Kennon L. *Twelve Keys to an Effective Church.* San Francisco: Harper & Row, 1983. This is one of the early staples in church development that discusses twelve vital tips to church growth.*

Church Ad Project. Winsted, MN. 1-800-331-9391. Catalog of advertising tools for evangelism.

Hadaway, C. Kirk. *Behold I Do a New Thing.* Cleveland: Pilgrim Press, 2001. One of the best resources available to help churches understand what their real purpose is—being a transformative community of faith.*

Hamilton, Adam. *Leading Beyond the Walls.* Nashville: Abingdon, 2002. Written by one of America's most successful contemporary pastors, this book seeks to lead congregations in developing a heart for the unchurched.

Hill, Robert L. *The Complete Guide to Small Group Ministry.* Boston: Skinner House Books, 2003. A practical guide to getting small (covenant) groups started in the church.

Hunter, George G. III. *Church for the Unchurched*. Nashville: Abingdon, 1996. Discusses proper goals for "apostolic churches," principles of outreach, and ways of communicating the gospel.

Johnson, Douglas W. *Vitality Means Church Growth*. Nashville: Abingdon, 1989. Outlines characteristics of vital churches.

Logan, Bob. *Beyond Church Growth*. Grand Rapids: Fleming H. Revell, 1989. Discusses the importance of visioning, characteristics of effective leaders, coaching, developing a philosophy, characteristics of vital worship, cell group network, mobilizing according to spiritual gifts.

McGavran, Donald A., and Winfield C. Arn. *Ten Steps for Church Growth*. Nashville: Discipleship Resources, 1977. One of the earlier works that gives an introduction to biblical church growth principles.

Miller, Herb. *How to Build a Magnetic Church*. Nashville: Abingdon, 1987. Lists numerous characteristics that help make churches "magnetic."*

Reese, Martha Grace. *Unbinding the Gospel: Real Life Evangelism*. St. Louis: Chalice Press, 2006. Based on the studies of 150 mainline churches and interviews with over a thousand people.

Schaller, Lyle E. *44 Steps Up Off the Plateau*. Nashville: Abingdon, 1993. Lists common church plateaus, why churches plateau, and strategies for getting over the attendance plateaus.

Schaller, Lyle E. *44 Ways to Increase Church Attendance*. Nashville: Abingdon, 1988. Lists forty-four practical tips for increasing overall attendance.*

Schaller, Lyle E. *Growing Plans*. Nashville: Abingdon, 1983. Lists hindrances to growth and strategies for growth.

Schwarz, Christian A. *The ABC's of Natural Church Development.* St. Charles, IL: Church Smart Resources, 1998. Lists eight quality characteristics of growing churches and how to identify your church's weakest characteristic, which is an impediment to growth.

Shumate, Charles R. *Bring a Friend Day Manual.* Anderson, IN: Church Extension and Home Missions, 1988. Excellent resource for helping churches plan a successful "Friend Day."

Southerland, Dan. *Transitioning: Leading Your Church through Change.* Grand Rapids: Zondervan, 1999. One of the newer, good resources in assisting churches in discovering, casting, and implementing God's vision for the church.

Wagner, C. Peter. *Your Church Can Be Healthy.* Nashville: Abingdon, 1979. One of the older resources that lists various diseases that affect churches and impede growth and how to diagnose them.

Wagner, C. Peter. *Your Church Can Grow.* Ventura, CA: Regal Books, 1976. Lists seven vital signs of a healthy church.

Warren, Rick. *The Purpose Driven Church.* Grand Rapids: Zondervan, 1995. One of the best works available in helping churches design a statement of purpose.*

NEW CHURCH START RESOURCES

A Guidebook for Planting New Congregations in the United Church of Christ. Cleveland: Evangelism Ministry Team, 2005.*

Kimball, Dan. *The Emerging Church: Vintage Christianity for New Generations.* Grand Rapids: Zondervan, 2003.

Nebel, Tom, and Gary Rohrmayer. *Church Planting Landmines.* Saint Charles, IL: Church Smart Resources, 2005.

Schaller, Lyle E. *44 Questions for Church Planters*. Nashville: Abingdon, 1991. Tested advice based on more than thirty years of working with leaders responsible for developing new churches. Where to begin, what works best, mission and identity, location, finances, and other topics are addressed.*

Tinsley, William. *Upon This Rock: Dimensions of Church Planting*. Atlanta: Southern Baptist Convention, 1985. Speaks of the importance of relationships and compassion, networks, characteristics of effective leaders.

Whitesel, Bob. *Inside the Organic Church: Learning from 12 Emerging Congregations*. Nashville: Abingdon, 2006. An in-depth study of twelve of more than forty of the so-called emerging churches that are popping up all over the world that were studied by the author.*

Wood, H. Stanley, ed. *Extraordinary Leaders in Extraordinary Times*. Grand Rapids: William B. Eerdman's, 2006.*

*Highly recommended

Note: Most of the recommended resources under the General Church Growth and Development heading are also recommended for those planting new churches.